UNDERSTANDING KATE ATKINSON

UNDERSTANDING CONTEMPORARY BRITISH LITERATURE

Matthew J. Bruccoli, Series Editor

Also of Interest

Understanding Alan Sillitoe, by Gillian Mary Hanson
Understanding Beryl Bainbridge, by Brett Josef Grubisic
Understanding Graham Greene, by R. H. Miller
Understanding Graham Swift, by David Malcolm
Understanding Ian McEwan, by David Malcolm
Understanding Jonathan Coe, by Merritt Moseley
Understanding Julian Barnes, by Merritt Moseley
Understanding Paul West, by David W. Madden
Understanding Penelope Fitzgerald, by Peter Wolfe
Understanding Tim Parks, by Gillian Fenwick

UNDERSTANDING

Kate Atkinson

Brian Diemert

THE UNIVERSITY OF
SOUTH CAROLINA PRESS

Published by the University of South Carolina Press
Columbia, South Carolina 29208

www.uscpress.com

Manufactured in the United States of America

29 28 27 26 25 24 23 22 21
10 9 8 7 6 5 4 3 2

Library of Congress Cataloging-in-Publication Data
can be found at http://catalog.loc.gov/.

ISBN 978-1-64336-152-9 (hardback)
ISBN 978-1-64336-153-6 (paperback)
ISBN 978-1-64336-154-3 (ebook)

CONTENTS

SERIES EDITOR'S PREFACE

The volumes of Understanding Contemporary British Literature have been planned as guides or companions for students as well as good nonacademic readers. The editor and publisher perceive a need for these volumes because much of the influential contemporary literature makes special demands. Uninitiated readers encounter difficulty in approaching works that depart from the traditional forms and techniques of prose and poetry. Literature relies on conventions, but the conventions keep evolving; new writers form their own conventions—which in time may become familiar. Put simply, UCBL provides instruction in how to read certain contemporary writers—identifying and explicating their material, themes, use of language, point of view, structures, symbolism, and responses to experience.

The word *understanding* in the titles was deliberately chosen. Many willing readers lack an adequate understanding of how contemporary literature works—that is, what the author is attempting to express and the means by which it is conveyed. Although the criticism and analysis in the series have been aimed at a level of general accessibility, these introductory volumes are meant to be applied in conjunction with the works they cover. They do not provide a substitute for the works and authors they introduce but rather prepare the reader for more profitable literary experiences.

M.J.B.

ACKNOWLEDGMENTS

While preparing this book on Kate Atkinson's work, I had the support of many people who need to be acknowledged and thanked. Thanks are due to the anonymous readers and editors, especially Aurora Bell, at the University of South Carolina Press, and to many of my colleagues at Brescia University College in London, Ontario, who have been helpful through conversation and encouragement. I am especially indebted to Dr. Monika Lee for her unwavering assistance, encouragement, and love. Our daughters Anna Lee-Diemert and Natasha Lee-Diemert also deserve thanks; they are constant reminders of what really matters. This book is in memory of my parents, Marvin Diemert (1935–2003) and Barbara Diemert (1937–2019), who knew the book was coming but sadly would not see it in print.

ONE

Understanding Kate Atkinson

Kate Atkinson released her eleventh novel, *Big Sky,* in June 2019, and her critical reputation continues to grow. A cursory glance at her career shows she has received considerable praise over the last twenty-five years, and her books routinely appear on best of the year lists. She occupies, as Jonathan Dee (2018) notes, "that rare cultural sweet spot wherein she scoops up awards for artistic excellence while also reliably hitting the best-seller lists." It is no surprise, then, to see that she has written books in several genres, some of which, including mysteries, are associated with commercial success. Indeed, her career can be considered, so far, as falling into three phases: her first three novels are standalone stories of families and their secrets; her next four novels are mysteries featuring investigator Jackson Brodie (*Big Sky* is a fifth Brodie book), and three of her most recent novels deal with aspects of the Second World War. Atkinson has also published in various places a book of thematically linked short stories, a play, and other short stories, including a small gathering of three Christmas-themed stories appeared in the fall of 2019 for charity under the title *Festive Spirits.* She would be the first to say that generic distinctions in her body of work are meaningless because shifting narrative time frames and recurring themes of family relations and buried secrets have always featured in her work.

Emma Parker, in her discussion of *Behind the Scenes at the Museum* in what is to this point the only monograph devoted to Atkinson's work, admirably introduces the basic concerns and themes of that novel and points to their continuance in *Human Croquet* and *Emotionally Weird.* She also describes reviewers' receptions of *Behind the Scenes at the Museum* and especially the negative turn that published comment took after that novel won the Whitbread Award (Parker 2002, 74–82). Atkinson has since won the same prize twice more (for *Life After Life* and *A God in Ruins;* the name of the award was changed in 2006 to the Costa Book Award) and is now secure in her reputation as a leading British author. In 1995, however, things were decidedly different. As Parker enumerates, the book was well received, but when it won over Salman Rushdie's *The Moor's Last Sigh* and Roy Jenkins's *Gladstone* (both were favored), critical comment in the press turned to reveal a surprising degree of prejudice from otherwise respected commentators. "Richard Hoggart, chairman of the Whitbread judges, said that Atkinson had written a Post-Modern novel, but might not know it" (Mantel 1996)—a comment betraying not only sexism but ignorance of Atkinson. Hilary Mantel came to Atkinson's defense and condemned the "sexist bigotry that still beleaguers women writers" (Parker 2002, 77): "Was this 1996? One felt spun back in time to, say, 1956" (Mantel 1996).

Kate Atkinson was born in York, England, in 1951 where her family ran a medical and surgical supplies shop. She recalled, "I was solitary, never happy. Without siblings you get quite a skewed vision of yourself and of the world. . . . I remember feeling quite lonely. My father was an autodidact. It wasn't a middle-class house. Shopkeepers were aspirant. He paid for me to go to private school. He was denied an education—he had a horrible childhood" (Fox 2011). She read voraciously, mentioning Lewis Carroll's Alice books consistently in interviews and commentary. Indeed, Emma Parker reports that Atkinson "re-read [*Alice in Wonderland*] every week between the ages of five and ten" (Parker 2002, 22)—surely not literally true.

Atkinson attended Queen Anne Grammar School for Girls in York. In 1970 she entered Dundee University where she studied English literature and, at twenty-one in 1973, married a fellow student and had her first daughter, Eve, the next year. At Dundee she completed her undergraduate degree and masters' degree in 1974. Those who suspected Atkinson of a blindness to postmodernism in *Behind the Scenes at the Museum* were surely in the dark, for Atkinson—as is now well reported, though the details are sketchy—had completed a doctoral dissertation titled "The Post-Modern American Short Story in Its Historical Context" at Dundee, but she was refused at the *viva*—an almost impossible situation in many universities. "Atkinson believes interdepartmental politics played their part, and the injustice still rankles," Alex Clark reported in 2001; but she has also linked the birth of her first daughter to the difficulties with the doctorate—"I thought doing a doctorate and having a baby would be a good combination. Actually, having a baby isn't a good combination with anything" (Clark 2001). Ten years later, in a different interview, Atkinson, newly awarded a MBE (Member of the Most Excellent Order of the British Empire), noted that Dundee had offered her an honorary degree: "I wrote a polite letter saying no thank you"; she wants the real thing: "Before I die I want someone to say 'Dr Atkinson'" (Fox 2011). There's little doubt that if Atkinson's dissertation ever is published or made available to scholars, it will provide an interesting gloss on her fiction. As it is, she has often commented on Donald Barthelme and Robert Coover, two of the authors she studied, along with Ronald Sukenick, Steve Katz, and John Barth (Parker 2002, 25), and she has written an introduction to the Penguin reissue of Coover's *Pricksongs and Descants.* She alludes to both Barthelme and Coover in some of her early work.[1] Atkinson is clear in an interview with Fiona Tolan: "I was very influenced by the stuff I did for my doctorate, by [Donald] Barthelme and [Robert] Coover—Coover particularly" (2008, 6).

Obviously, the collapse of the doctorate proved a crisis, as did the dissolution of her marriage, but Atkinson is sanguine about the academic road not taken: "If I had got my doctorate I wouldn't have become a writer. Had I continued I would probably be studying something like passivity and activity in the language of Jane Austen" (Teeman 2008). A second marriage in 1982 provided another daughter, Helen, but also ended in divorce. Currently living in Edinburgh, Atkinson is fiercely protective of her privacy, especially as it relates to her family. What is known of her life, as we've seen, is revealed sporadically in promotional interviews, and Parker's text summarizes a good bit of that information.

Parker's guide to Atkinson's first novel focuses on that book, but the useful discussion ranges over themes and ideas that are evident in all of Atkinson's writing, although Parker's text, published in 2002, can only acknowledge the first three novels, some short stories, and Atkinson's play, *Abandonment* (2000). Parker did offer some speculations about possible future projects, but none have proved accurate. Since then Atkinson's work has moved in other directions, with a collection of linked short fiction, a series of detective novels, and three more historically focused books. Her most recent novel, *Big Sky,* returns to the detective series, which proved very popular and has been adapted for television; indeed, the last episodes in the second season of *Case Histories* (the first Brodie novel's title, standing for all of the television presentations) do continue beyond the end of *Started Early, Took My Dog* (2010), but those narratives are not picked up in *Big Sky.* As Arthur Conan Doyle and Ian Rankin both realized, it is very difficult to "retire" a popular investigator; Brodie, Atkinson once said, was "not dead, merely parked somewhere" (Butki 2011). *Big Sky* takes place almost ten years after the events in the previous installment, *Started Early, Took My Dog,* which I discuss later, and a few characters from the earlier Brodie novels return while the possibility for further Jackson Brodie novels remains: "I don't see any reason why you shouldn't return to characters all the time. . . . I wish I'd done it earlier, I wish I'd kept on returning to characters in my books. It would have been quite interesting, you get such shift in development" (Jewell 2008). The point applies equally well to members of the Todd family in *Life After Life* and *A God in Ruins.*

From a broader perspective, we can see that in all of Atkinson's work there are numerous narrative strands within a single text. In *A God in Ruins,* Teddy is the central figure, but we remember him from *Life After Life,* where his story unfolds in different directions depending on which path his sister Ursula's life takes. Ursula Todd is central in *Life After Life,* but her existence is constantly and fractally repeated. In the short story collection *Not the End of the World,* characters overlap and cross into various stories. The play, *Abandonment,* runs parallel narratives, separated by more than a century but occurring in the same house. A featured trope of postmodernism is that narratives proliferate in unpredictable ways and are often playful, even fantastic: in postmodernism, Atkinson says, "the pretense of 'reality' was abandoned, along with an attempt at extracting meaning" (Atkinson, Introduction to *Pricksongs,* v–vi). Hence, reviewers and critics are sometimes at a loss when trying to categorize her work. Is *Human Croquet,* to take one response, "magical post-modern metafiction? post-magical realism/post-modern magicalism" (Weber 1997)? Atkinson knows all of this and saw it in work by Barth, Barthelme, Coover, Kurt Vonnegut, and others. Yet the strain of the fantastic in her work is not only attributable to postmodernism. Several influences are apparent, some of which are easily guessed at from a very few pages of *Behind the Scenes at the Museum.* Aside from recalling Laurence Sterne's *Tristram Shandy,* the opening pages also allude to Jane Austen, Shakespeare, Henry James, and Lewis Carroll. Atkinson offered her own top-ten list in the *Guardian* in 2000, and it is easy to see how the many first-person narrators in her list (Nick Carraway, John Dowell, Humbert Humbert, Huck Finn, etc.) would be relevant to the narration of *Behind the Scenes at the Museum,* with Ruby's evasions, ignorance, and misunderstanding being central to that book's power.[2] *Human Croquet* and *Emotionally Weird* also employ first-person narration, but none of her other novels do.

The intertextual range in Atkinson's texts is impressive but never alienating; as Katharine Weber wrote in her review of *Human Croquet,* "it really doesn't matter if a reader recognizes every gesture in Atkinson's literary high-wire act, because the multitude of characters are defined with such vivid specificity that they—and what happens to them—matter the most." The stories are compelling and often moving; several scenes are emotionally powerful, despite linguistic playfulness and textual self-consciousness. Of course, recognizing allusions is fun, and they do add meaning to what we read while undercutting canonical distinctions, but Atkinson remains accessible. "I do like character, and I do like plot. . . . I like narrative—the satisfaction of narrative" (Tolan 2008, 6–7). Atkinson's world is that of York and Britain, their people and their history. Indeed, as *Behind the Scenes at the Museum* evinces, twentieth-century Britain, especially its experience of the Second World War, provides rich material for re-envisioning history. *Life After Life* is perhaps most explicit in this enterprise, but all her books engage the project, including the Brodie novels, the first of which, *Case Histories* (2004), weaves intersecting crimes decades apart into Brodie's present moment.

Atkinson's broad appeal, for some critics, has caused her books to be dismissed as "middlebrow" fiction, which is never a compliment. The term emerged in the 1920s as the necessary medium between "highbrow" and "lowbrow," which both came into use prior to the First World War. Although tainted with their associations with nineteenth-century "racial science," these descriptors were quickly adopted to describe taste distinctions among readers and writers. While one might use the pages of lowbrow publications to line a birdcage, more discerning readers preserved highbrow material for rereading. "But what," Virginia Woolf pondered, "is a middlebrow? And that, to tell the truth, is no easy question to answer. They are neither one thing nor the other. . . . The middlebrow is the man, or woman, of middlebred intelligence who ambles and saunters now on this side of the hedge, now on that, in pursuit of no single object, neither art itself nor life itself, but both mixed indistinguishably, and rather nastily, with money, fame, power, or prestige" (1961, 155). In literary terms, this view has found a most charitable champion in Nicola Humble: "the middlebrow novel is one that straddles the divide between the trashy romance or the thriller on the one hand, and the philosophically or formally challenging novel on the other: offering narrative excitement without guilt, and intellectual stimulation without undue effort" (2001, 11). The concept is also often presented as a gendered term. That is, fiction that appeals to or is written by women is often discussed as "middlebrow" (Humble's book is about the "feminine middlebrow novel"[3]). Roger Luckhurst, whose influential book *The Trauma Question* I will return to, groups *Behind the Scenes at the Museum* with a number of novels (Jane Smiley's *A Thousand Acres,* Nicci French's *The Memory Game*) as a mainstream text that demonstrates how formalized the conventions of trauma fiction became in the 1990s. Luckhurst shiftily remarks of Atkinson's novel and the others that "one might be tempted to call these works less mainstream than middlebrow, were this not such a loaded term. Middlebrow is always pejorative, coined . . . to describe a largely feminine, middle-class, safely unexperimental, commercial, and critically ignored writing" (2008, 110). One suspects that it is Atkinson's accessibility, her popularity, that stimulates the desire to account for her appeal in such a way that her work is diminished.

Atkinson's early success was often presented as coming out of nowhere; Hoggart, we recall, couldn't imagine that Atkinson would be familiar with postmodernism. When she won the Whitbread Prize, newspaper commentary emphasized her status as a single mother who once worked as hotel housekeeper. (A similar narrative was retailed for J. K. Rowling—the single mother on social assistance whose books made her one of the world's richest women.) The emphasis on such modest beginnings, of course, conveys dual and contradictory messages. On the one hand, humble beginnings need not prevent one's success, but on the other, such success is surprising because it is found among those who are supposed ignorant and so, in this regard, perhaps undeserving. Neither position credits the author with intelligence, imagination, knowledge, or talent (even though both Atkinson and Rowling are university educated), and, although Atkinson did work as a chambermaid for a short time as summer employment (as does Ruby in *Behind the Scenes at the Museum* and as did Juliet Armstrong in *Transcription*—more fuel for biographical speculation), she also taught English at Dundee, where she earned two degrees and nearly a third. (Rowling is a graduate of Exeter, where she studied Classics and French.)

Attempts to disparage Atkinson's award and her work early in her career reflect the prejudices of an old boy's network; as Hilary Mantel (1996) notes: "There is a double standard operating here. 'Never,' [Atkinson] has written, 'have my hair, my nails, my clothes, my marital status been of as much interest to anyone as they were to the women of the London press.' The *Sunday Times* quoted Anita Brookner recently: 'I think literature is without gender.' Think again. Hundreds of thousands of words have been written about Salman Rushdie—and we know nothing of his manicure." Ten years later Atkinson remained convinced that any controversy that arose after her award stemmed from the fact that she is a woman: "I think most of the literary prizes are won by men. If you look at . . . the Booker and the Whitbread, it's mostly men who've won them, especially the Booker: it's a boy's prize. . . . We live in an incredibly sexist society, we just don't see it anymore because it's so subtle" (Tolan 2008, 4).[4] In recent years, the success of *Life After Life* and *A God in Ruins* seems to have quieted those critical voices. Still, the assumption for some reviewers is that Atkinson built her readership for these novels out of her success with genre fiction: the Brodie novels were not considered literary fiction on the level with her other books, even though she was seen to stretch but not break the genre's confines.[5] Atkinson dismisses labels for her books, and describes her writing method in the most casual of terms: "I don't have goals when writing books apart from getting to the end. I have rather vague ideas about how I want things to feel, I'm big on ambience. I have a title, a beginning and a probable ending and go from there. Writing for me is quite a plastic form, a kind of mental sculpture. . . . It acquires its character and its depth as it goes along" (Butki 2011). Elsewhere, she says, "I don't plan books: because if I knew what happened, why would I write it?" (Tolan 2008, 10). Some of this might be disingenuous, but it is certainly not unusual for writers to talk about the writing process as one of discovery and not the direct transcription of a preconceived arc. Atkinson's books, however, are often praised for their tightly woven plots, so to dismiss the idea of planning may be misleading, but this doesn't mean everything falls to preconceived endings.

My discussion of Atkinson's fiction breaks neatly along the natural divisions of her career as a writer. The opening section deals with her first three novels, *Behind the Scenes at the Museum* (1995), *Human Croquet* (1997), and *Emotionally Weird* (2000), which were all heavily marked by Atkinson's reading and display a playfulness in plot and discourse, to say nothing of their humor. Each first-person narrator (to this point the only examples in her oeuvre) is a young woman seeking to understand her family's history, her origins, and, in turn, herself. Each, as Atkinson noted later, is "based on *Alice in Wonderland* in one way or another—but the young girls has now reached 21 and is grown up" (Bunce 2000). Atkinson later felt constrained by the kind of fiction she'd been writing and so shifted her attentions to a series of linked short stories and a play. She has often returned to the short story form, which inaugurated her career as a writer, but many of her stories are difficult to find, so I have confined my discussion to those gathered in *Not the End of the World* (2002). Similarly, space doesn't permit a full discussion of her play, *Abandonment* (2000), so my focus is restricted to her readily available prose fiction. The play, however, does connect thematically with Atkinson's other work and is part of the transitional phase of her career. The series of detective novels, featuring Jackson Brodie (2004–10; 2019) reflect another direction for her writing and contributed greatly to her popularity with readers. Since 2013 three novels outside of the Brodie series have appeared, *Life After Life* (2013), *A God in Ruins* (2015), and *Transcription* (2018), all dealing with aspects of the Second World War. Consequently, this study falls into four unequal parts that explore Atkinson's development as a writer. Of course, because she is a contemporary novelist, it is impossible to predict the ultimate shape of her career, so all that follows can only be provisional.

TWO

A Postmodern Trilogy?

Behind the Scenes at the Museum, Human Croquet, and *Emotionally Weird*

Atkinson's first three books, because they have been around longer, have provoked the most academic criticism, including the only monograph on her work—Emma Parker's *Reader's Guide to "Behind the Scenes at the Museum"* (2002). *Behind the Scenes at the Museum, Human Croquet,* and *Emotionally Weird* have sometimes been thought of as a loose trilogy (even Atkinson has referred to them that way [Bunce 2000]). The impulse to see them as a unit derives from commonalities among the narrating voices and shared thematic strands, such as the relationships of mothers and daughters. As well, their self-consciousness and a high degree of allusiveness, which foreground their status as literary texts, implicitly free them from the demands of verisimilitude because, in the literary universe, anything is possible. Equally a factor in how we might consider these three novels as a grouping is that Atkinson looked to "[break] out of a straitjacket" with the short stories that followed in *Not the End of the World.* Her fourth novel, then, shifted the genre from the family romance to the crime story, inaugurating a series featuring Jackson Brodie, a former police officer and now private investigator. Although Atkinson's career neatly breaks into phases, several continuities mean the transition from *Human Croquet* and *Emotionally Weird* to *Case Histories* is less abrupt than it might first appear. Indeed, *Emotionally Weird* toys with the detective genre in the character of Chick, a former village policeman and now a private detective, and in the narrator Effie's crime story for her creative writing class.

Behind the Scenes at the Museum

Behind the Scenes at the Museum is a coming-of-age story but also about "working-class life in York over three generations" (Aitkenhead 1996) and much more. And it isn't autobiography, despite some details. On a basic level, the story centers on Ruby Lennox and her family, consisting of three sisters—Patricia, Gillian, and Pearl, and her parents, Bunty and George. On another level the novel develops the history of Ruby's maternal ancestors back into the nineteenth century in a series of chapters described as "Footnotes."[1] As a first novel, *Behind the Scenes at the Museum* established a narrative method that Atkinson would develop over the next decades. Innocuous objects (such as a button, a teaspoon, a rabbit's foot) recur throughout the novel to knit generations and narrative strands. Phrasing and allusion, too, are repeated while at a larger level, narrative preoccupations (relationships among women and generations of family, the mysteries of the past, myths about motherhood, and the spaces between appearances and reality) continue in later texts. Similarly, the question of what the "right" life one is to live—Alice, Nell, Bunty, and Ruby all believe at different points in *Behind the Scenes at the Museum* that the life they are in is not the "right" one—remains unanswered. And at the core of *Behind the Scenes at the Museum,* as in her other books, is a central trauma that the narrative hints at before confronting.

In this last regard, *Behind the Scenes at the Museum* reflects on one level the cultural preoccupation with recovered memories of the late 1980s and early 1990s. That is, individuals in analysis discover that entirely forgotten events actually occurred and that those events may account for aspects of or behaviors in their lives. The debate about "recovered" memories soon evolved into concerns about false memory syndrome and the idea of recovered memories became a site of controversy (Luckhurst 2008, 107). Nonetheless, the notion that an individual could be entirely ignorant of traumatic experience proved fruitful for fiction where standards of veracity are perhaps less consequential. As is the case in Jane Smiley's *A Thousand Acres* (1991), trauma underscores the narrative in *Behind the Scenes at the Museum.* In Ruby's case, the death of her twin sister, Pearl, and Ruby's presumed responsibility for it, constitute the central event that colors her perceptions, although she is unaware of that being the case. Consequently, the hostility the narrator, Ruby, expresses toward her sister Gillian may be due to something other than a clash of personalities.[2] Gillian, we learn, coaxed the four-year-old Pearl on to the ice of a frozen pond, and she broke through. Gillian then blamed the accident on Ruby, saying that Ruby had pushed Pearl. Gillian, who is only about three years older than Ruby and Pearl, is, except for one moment late in the book, never presented sympathetically, and her own early death at the age of twelve (she is killed by a car on Christmas Eve 1959, when she runs across a busy street after leaving a theater) is mentioned often in Ruby's account before we actually hear the details of the accident. There is, however, no explicit revelation or even mention of Pearl's existence until late in the book. Ruby's forecasting of Gillian's death, though, is marked by cool and detached phrasing: "Make the most of it, I say," Ruby imagines in response to Gillian's yelling at the performance; "'Really, she *is* a one, our Gillian' [Bunty says]. Not for much longer" (163); "[Bunty] is making a big mistake, she's hanging onto the wrong child [Ruby]" (165). The contrast between the ways Ruby deals with each of her sisters' deaths is striking.

The construction of the narrator here was particularly challenging for Atkinson because Ruby as the narrator stands apart from the world she inhabits. Her language, knowledge of the future, and cool wit all position her as a mature individual who, we must conclude, can only imagine the lives of her ancestors in the "Footnote" sections and in the prenatal life she describes in the opening chapter. Atkinson's book opens with a nod to Laurence Sterne and *Tristram Shandy,* as Ruby describes her conception and gestation in Bunty's womb. Filled with questions that often prove to have tremendous bearing on the story—for instance, "Will [Gillian] be a good sister? Is this a good mother?" (20); "And why do I have this strange feeling, as if my shadow's stitched to my back, almost as if there's someone else in here with me? Am I being haunted by my own embryonic ghost?" (16–17)—this first chapter reveals details of the past, the present, and the future (Gillian's death, for example [19]). The range of allusions in the discourse—Sterne, Defoe, Chekov, Gary Cooper, *Gone With the Wind, The Wizard of Oz,* "Go ask Alice" (24, which itself goes in at least four directions), Munch, Quattrocento (and perhaps through that one to Yeats), to pick up some of the more obvious ones—expresses Atkinson's ludic impulses and makes it difficult to account for Ruby's narrating stance.[3] Conceived on the opening day of 1951's Festival of Britain, Ruby will narrate her life in relation to particular years and events in Britain's second half of the twentieth century. In this way, Atkinson can probe the history of Britain and contrast that public history with the domestic history of Ruby, her family, and her extended family.[4]

Much of the book's encounter with the British past is revealed in the "Footnotes" sections of the novel. This designation, as Fiona Tolan, Emma Parker, and others have noted, points to the marginal status of feminine domestic history—the stories told not in but behind the museum that is the archive of the official past. The Footnotes sections tell of Ruby's great-grandmother Alice, her children (one of whom is Nell, Ruby's grandmother), and grandchildren, one of whom is Bunty (born Berenice [11]). Ruby admits that what she writes in these sections is imagined. Looking at a photograph from 1888 of Alice and her children born to that point, Ruby imagines: "I want to rescue this lost woman from what's going to happen to her (time). Dive into the picture pluck her out—*Picture the scene—*" (29). As Ruby says in the first couple of pages, "Who is to say which of these is real and which a fiction?" (12).

So, how reliable is Ruby? She obviously conceals things or, rather, half reveals them. Her sleepwalking, nightmares ("terrible dream of drowning, of falling, of being trapped, of flying" [109] and, later, about "the end of the world" [188]), and frequent references to ghosts all betray things we (and she?) don't quite understand. Atkinson's treatment of Ruby's narration is subtle and deceptive. For one thing, Ruby generally narrates events in the present tense, so her childhood and growing up have an immediacy for us. On the other hand, she clearly possesses a knowledge of things to come, such as Gillian's early death, that position her outside the immediate circumstances of her youth. This distancing contributes to and may indeed account for Ruby's ironical and detached tone. Similarly the Footnotes sections narrate a family history that Ruby can only conjecture about well after the dated chapters recording her development. All this suggests that she is also aware that she is a twin and of the circumstances of her twin sister Pearl's death. For the first time reader, these revelations come as a surprise but, as one would expect, are hinted at in numerous places to be recognized later.

The most explicit indications are offered in chapter 4, "1956 The Naming of Things," which recounts four-year-old Ruby's mysterious exile to her Aunt Bab's in Dewsbury. Here Ruby's unnamed fears come to the fore, but when she attends a spiritualist gathering with her aunt, Ruby receives a message: "*Your sister says not to worry about her,* and Auntie Babs gives a little gasp" (108). Ruby ponders the message and worries about her older sisters, Patricia and Gillian (109). Shortly afterward, Ruby spells "Pearl" on a Ouija board (112). While explicit—Ruby has a dead sister named Pearl—the sources of the information prevents readers from giving it credence. The four-year-old Ruby, who is trying to teach herself to read (or is it the older narrating Ruby's spelling of the name?), of course, expresses no conscious memory of Pearl (and so tends to see photographs of Pearl as being of herself), but the older narrating Ruby surely knows why there seem to be twice as many photos of her than there are of Patricia or Gillian in the "framed Polyphotos" (80). The 1956 chapter, as Tracy Hargreaves notes (2009), is rife with allusions and references to doublings and pairings from which Ruby is excluded. Her aunt's house reminds her of "above the shop" (104) where she lives; Auntie Babs, like her younger sister Bunty, is "also a slave to housework" (106) and she has twin daughters, Daisy and Rose (named for flowers, just as Ruby and Pearl are named for jewels). Phrases and sounds, too, are often repeated: "Ready, Teddy—steady, Teddy—Go!" (105). There's also a double bed and a "huge, double-fronted wardrobe and matching dressing table" (103) in the room she's sleeping in with her twin cousins. There's also a "big four-storey Victorian" doll's house that mirrors in a shrunken fashion the world she's in and so she fears getting trapped inside it (104). (In a moment of mature clarity, Ruby wonders if Bunty is also trapped in a doll's house, and describes the thought as Ibsenesque [107]). When she returns home, "I go to sleep in my own bed for the first time in what seems like a long time. It's strange to be alone in my bedroom and I have a distinct feeling that something—or somebody—is missing. . . . Why do I have such unquiet sleep? Something has changed" (113). When she arrived home, Bunty clarified, "'we're all going to try and carry on and put the accident behind us.' Well, that's fine by me, seeing as I have no idea what 'accident' she's talking about" (112). The fact that the young Ruby fails to acknowledge Pearl consciously until quite late in the book (chapter 11, "1968 Wisdom") after a quarrel with Mr. Belling (285–88) means that to this point Pearl has been an absent presence in Ruby's life and in the discourse. From Atkinson's point of view, the trick is to keep Pearl's existence hidden, yet available when readers reach the novel's end. It is a bit of a narrative game, but to say that in no way diminishes the emotional impact of the discovery. Textual game play is central to much of the postmodern fiction Atkinson studied, of course, and the concept of gaming is explicit in the title of her next novel, *Human Croquet,* but the challenge is more than play. The question is, how is trauma to be narrated?

Pearl's hidden presence points to one way in which the trauma narrative can be constructed. For many commentators such as Mieke Bal (1999), Ernst van Alphen (1999), and Anne Whitehead (2004), trauma defies narrative. Roger Luckhurst, working from Cathy Caruth and Sigmund Freud, discusses trauma as "an aporia in narrative" (2008, 81, 83): "trauma is a crisis of representation, . . . this generates narrative *possibility* just as much as *impossibility,* a compulsive outpouring of attempts to formulate narrative knowledge," which goes some way toward explaining Ruby's "Footnotes" and the attempt to reinscribe the lost and missing members of her family history. Luckhurst reductively sees *Behind the Scenes at the Museum* as a kind of "middlebrow" novel that uses the trauma narrative without fully engaging its complexities. As he sees it, the trauma narrative became formalized: "narrative anachrony [a disruption in the chronological ordering of events] as a symptom of buried trauma; belated revelation that regressively rewrites the significance of motifs; discordance that is reintegrated to find different levels of concordant narrative coherence" (105). Such a reading, while partly valid, does no justice to Atkinson, who, while self-consciously recognizing narrative's power to create a world ("words are the only things that can construct a world that makes sense" [*Behind the Scenes* 332]), sees trauma as inexpressible—surely one of the reasons we hear nothing about Pearl's death until late in the book. Gillian's death, by way of contrast, is not only forecasted but clearly described. The chapter "Wisdom," in which Pearl's death is revealed, is fragmentary and chronologically disruptive; that is, we understand that a miserable Ruby has attempted suicide, so she now is with Dr. Hezmark.[5] Then we find out about her "scene" with Belling (a character who is mentioned in the first lines of the novel). Even the word "scene" masks the depth of what is revealed because it implies an argument that might be regarded as insignificant, even typical, given Belling's status as Bunty's new boyfriend. (Belling has already taken it upon himself to discipline Ruby for her backtalk to her mother [279].) So in the word *scene* we recognize evidence of the repression that pervades Ruby's narrative. Belling views Ruby as a spoiled, sulky, and hostile teenager lacking parental discipline. His cruelly delivered revelation that she killed her sister is inspired by spite and occurs without Bunty's knowledge (to her credit, Bunty ends her relationship with Belling because of his treatment of Ruby). Ruby cannot deal with this incomplete knowledge, which accounts for her suicide attempt, because, if it is true, her entire understanding of herself and of her past is fundamentally altered. Nothing is the same. As Luckhurst observes, "the traumatic event confounds narrative knowledge" (2008, 88); it cannot be assimilated to ordinary experience because it is a rupture in "the assumptive world [which is the] illusion believed to be reality" (Kauffman 2002, 3). The trauma narrative, then, is marked by disruptions in linear time, the suspension of logical causation, and a kind of working backward toward the inaugurating traumatic event, among other things (Luckhurst 2008, 80). So how can one represent the overwhelming experience of trauma in any narrative, let alone fiction? As Hayden White and others have observed, fictions coordinate and arrange events within a structure of fulfillment (White 1985): expectations are met and endings are securely placed, but trauma "issues a challenge to the capacities of narrative knowledge . . . trauma is anti-narrative" (Luckhurst 2008, 79).

Historically, racial, national, and individual horrors have been experienced in incomprehensible forms, but trauma as a concept has been contested (Luckhurst 2008, 1–15): is it physiological, psychological, or both? What constitutes trauma and is traumatic? Is the same thing equally traumatic for all who experience it? Is it contagious? Can we speak of "transgenerational haunting"; that is, can trauma be passed on to later generations? (Luckhurst 2008, 69) (an interesting question in light of Ruby's family history). Whether one is witness to genocidal atrocity or a car accident (even a railway accident[6]), trauma can be experienced, and it can obviously involve whole populations (as with the Holocaust or Hiroshima). Ultimately, however, such moments depend upon their being shared discursively (van Alphen 1999, 37), which may or may not bring its own problems. In Ian McEwan's *The Child in Time* (1987), the aftermath of a traumatic event (the abduction of a toddler in a supermarket) remains an aporia, as the crime is never solved. The same cannot be said of Pearl's death, which is explained for Ruby and for readers, although there is no explicit mention that Bunty's understanding of the event is altered. In this sense the story of Pearl's fate continues to exist in different versions. Ruby's "recovered" memory absolves Ruby and is assumed to be "true" by the reader. That doesn't change Ruby's experience of the past or the things that shaped her upbringing except insofar as Ruby's narrative can take note of Bunty's pain. Bunty is never granted the interior consciousness that might allow us to sympathize with her, but the facts are that she had a philandering husband, two children die in childhood, a third run off, and the remaining one be deeply troubled. Bunty's life has clearly been difficult, and no material compensation can make up for that.[7] Ruby's response to Bunty's mourning appears callous but, of course, comes out of ignorance: "'My baby, my baby's gone,' as if she'd only had one baby, which wasn't very nice for me and Patricia. . . . Sometimes you could hear Bunty crying to the night, 'My Gillian, my pearl,' which I thought was very odd, because I'd never heard her call her that when she was alive. And anyway, surely it's me that's the jewel of the family?" (169). Later, we'll recognize the "My Gillian, my pearl" as a significant but overlooked clue in Ruby's narrative: the absence of the uppercase "P" conceals a truth while at the same time revealing it.

In considering *Behind the Scenes at the Museum* as a trauma narrative, a useful point of comparison might be Graham Swift's *Waterland* (1983) in which narrator Tom Crick works tirelessly to account for his wife, Mary's, inexplicable action of abducting a baby from a grocery store. Crick, a history teacher facing dismissal, ceaselessly burrows into the past to recount stories that seem to have bearing on the present, but explaining is, as his student Price says, "a way of avoiding the facts while you pretend to get near them" (145). Crick's narration can best be characterized as an example of "dissociation," which narrative theorist Mieke Bal, in her discussion of traumatic narration, contrasts with Freud's concept of repression insofar as "dissociation doubles the strand of the narrative series of events by splitting off a sideline" while "repression interrupts the flow of narratives that shape memory," creating ellipsis in the narrative which "stalls" the discursive process (van Alphen 1999, 27). In other words, "dissociation splits off material that cannot then be reincorporated into the main narrative" (Bal 1999, ix). Swift's book, like Atkinson's, narrates trauma through dissociation and repression. The "Footnotes" insertions in *Behind the Scenes at the Museum* are dissociative; they also "stall" the narrative by splitting events along a sideline while implying that a cause for present circumstances can be found in the family's past. In these novels, and this is true of many of Atkinson's books, events and time conspire to create an unredeemable moment that is suspended and apart from narrative while yet being integral to it.

The unredeemable moment is, of course, the place of trauma, which "cannot be integrated into diachrony, it is a blockage" (Luckhurst 2008, 81). Bal also speaks of the "blockage" as a "stutter" or, echoing Freud in "Beyond the Pleasure Principle," an unresolved repetition. In Atkinson's novel, the repeated hints of Pearl's absent presence are just such an unresolved repetition. Trauma is the gap within a narrative that resists narrative: "Traumatic memories remain present for the subject with particular vividness and/or totally resist integration. In both cases, they cannot become narrative" (Bal 1999, viii). Consequently, Pearl cannot appear, except obliquely, in Ruby's story. The frequently cited Cathy Caruth argues further that "traumatic experience . . . suggests a certain paradox that the most direct seeing of a violent event may occur as an absolute inability to know it" (1996, 91–91). Ruby does not "know" Pearl's death. And, as van Alphen adds, the event "depends on discourse to come about: forms of experience do not just depend on the event or history that is being experienced, but also on the discourse in which the event is expressed/thought/conceptualized" (1999, 24). In this sense, the event is already a representation because, as Bal said, "to enter memory, the traumatic event of the past needs to be narratable" (1999, x); hence the talking cure Ruby undertakes with Dr. Hezmark. In this respect, trauma lies outside narrative while also being the spur to narrative: "all literature is probably a version of the apocalypse. . . . Literature . . . represents the ultimate coding of our crises, of our most intimate and most serious apocalypses" (Kristeva 1982, 207–8). Disruption, as Todorov notes, forces narration (1977, 111): the quiet community that encounters the unexpected stranger; the sudden death in a family; the collapse of a marriage, fortune, structure; a stolen child—in each case, stories proliferate. Trauma's disruption in the ordinary course of life is felt in its aftermath: no one expects life's next moments to be irrevocably altering, but that is the traumatic moment when all preconceived narratives of the future are broken. Trauma breeches the divide between the inner life's expectation and the outer life's reality (Luckhurst 2008, 3): what is expected and imagined, if only in the banal anticipation of a future that is much like the present, is no longer possible. In a sense, two narratives, of the expected and the unexpected, of romance and irony, conflict to produce the space of trauma.

Ruby's trauma, while central, is far from the only catastrophic event in the book. Indeed, trauma seems so much a part of her family's history, especially her maternal family's, that the possibility of transgenerational wounding is entirely plausible. Of course, the two world wars frame the issue for the male members of her mother's family (as they do for characters in *Life After Life* and *A God in Ruins*), but the "Footnote" chapters reveal traces of continuities and resemblance across generations and so the search for origin is problematic. (Even Ruby's description of her conception, gestation, and birth points to the difficulties of locating a narrative of origins.) Perhaps ancestral pain can be traced back to Ruby's great-grandmother's desertion of her children, but one doubts that Alice Barker's actions can be considered the origin of Ruby's sorrows. It is even conceivable that family wounds preceded Alice's disappearance with Monsieur Armond, and there is a hint of this possibility in a brief mention of Alice's mother, Sophia, and her sister Hannah, who created a scandal by running off with a disgraced man; Hannah then lived in poverty while her sister Sophia married a wealthy older man and lived a privileged life until it was discovered that her husband was a criminal fraud, who then hanged himself.

Family fortunes collapsed and Sophia, Alice's mother, soon after also committed suicide, leaving Alice with nothing but "her mother's clock and a silver locket that her grandfather had given her when she was born" (31).[8] (Both the clock and the locket will return in the novel.)

It is difficult to account for Ruby's repression of Pearl's drowning—"Amnesia" (287), Bunty's explanation, which is accompanied by the further revelation that "of course we talked about her" (288)—almost seems too incredible: surely the four-year-old Ruby wouldn't have forgotten Pearl immediately, but in her recounting of her life from an undefined future position, she relies on memories that are fragmentary, distorted, and incomplete. Hence, she omits potentially painful details while casting others in a dubious light (Gillian, for example). Not only does she reveal the absent presence of Pearl throughout her account, but we must imagine that she is trying to hint at the knowledge she now (after the narrative) possesses while also trying to remain true to her own experience of ignorance. Apparently random details are left as breadcrumbs to mark a path toward a revelatory end. Even Ruby's twin cousins offer a clue: they are both named for flowers while a parallel set of twins, Ruby and Pearl, have similarly derived nomenclature, with names derived from gems. The difficulty is that the narrating Ruby, who can imagine her great-grandmother's life from scattered stories and photographs, hides her revelation of Pearl's existence even though she *must* know, unless we suppose another Ruby standing outside the narrative—which would make three, if we consider the youthful Ruby, the older narrating Ruby, and now a fully aware Ruby who takes over the last fifty pages or so.

Hilary Mantel (1996) saw "Atkinson's decision to prolong the narrative into Ruby's adulthood" as a "miscalculation": "Even this capacious book cannot contain it, and once the peak of intensity has passed, in Ruby's 16th year, neither we nor the author have the emotional energy to see her into the calm waters of middle age." Certainly the last section is literally anticlimactic, and events—even significant events—are narrated rapidly (chapters dated 1970 and 1992 cover a large range of experience, as Ruby finishes school, works in an Edinburgh hotel, gets married, has children, leaves her marriage, reconnects with Patricia, and recounts her mother's death). We also learn about Alice's life and what happened to her son, Lawrence, the child who saw her leave all those years before and who also ran away from home. All of this material, as well as details about the lives of friends (Kathleen) and extended family members (Adrian, Lucy-Vida), surfaces, but those stories remain untold. Atkinson has said that she likes the endings that narration can provide, so the closing off of narrative strands in these last pages satisfies readers' curiosity about lingering issues and answers questions about what happened to many of the characters. But in other ways, these last chapters address some of the book's motifs that are dwarfed by the powerful revelation of Pearl's existence and death. Indeed, we can easily feel that plot's resolution to be the overwhelming piece that has been missing, the part that explains everything we have wondered about Ruby. We find in the last forty or so pages that there has been more going on than we were aware of at the time. The footnote (XI) immediately following the full revelation about Pearl is called, "The wrong life," and it returns us to Alice's choice to desert her family for a life with Monsieur Armond. In her case, the decision to abandon her children is deeply regretted, and Atkinson—and Ruby—tie Alice's longing to find her children to the outbreak of the Great War, which prevents her return to England. As so many stories about that war recount, the mother becomes aware of one child's death (Albert, in this case) through his ghostly apparition when it happened (302). Chance and coincidence play a role years later in the search for her children when she unknowingly passes Nell with Clifford towing her grandchildren Bunty and Babs in a York street (304). Alice dies an old woman, in an air raid in 1940 in Sheffield, clutching a photograph of her children. This section tells us what happened to Alice, but it is frankly sentimental and, as with Alice's vision of the recently killed Albert, cliché ridden. This is, after all, Ruby's imagining and she adopts, as Isobel Fairfax does in *Human Croquet* when she tells of her Renaissance ancestors, familiar narrative patterns to fill out her accounts.

Ruby's life carried on, of course, after her suicide attempt, but like the other women in her maternal lineage, she felt she was "leading the wrong life," saying to her husband, Gian-Carlo, "You've got the wrong wife" (313). Her response, though, points to one of the reasons Atkinson continued the novel after the big revelation, and that is that Ruby breaks the self-destructive pattern of Alice and the other women: she takes her children, Alice and Pearl, with her. Indeed, this final section reminds us that there have been women who have found ways to make new lives for themselves. Patricia, for instance, who makes contact with Ruby after many years just prior to Ruby making her own decision to leave her husband, is married and living in Australia with her husband and two children. Patricia is also about to become a veterinarian (her childhood aspiration, although she forgets that [314]). Similarly, we recall that Bunty's sister, Betty, and before that Nell's sister, Lillian, had emigrated to Canada and had full lives there, and in Lillian's case, the family story is passed on through the wife, Tina Donner, of a grandson, Andy (272–73). Ruby and her children hardly go so far (they remain in Scotland), but these women have all found ways to establish new lives beyond the circumscriptions of their origins. The fact that Patricia, Ruby, and Bunty are reunited late in the book also reverses, as McDermott points out, the familial pattern of dispersed siblings (2006, 77). In fact, the narrative pulls together not only characters but narrative strands. In the final chapter, "1992 Redemption," the dying Bunty is attended by a nurse, "Sister Blake"

(Tessa), who had been given up by her young mother during the war. Several clues tell us that Tessa is the daughter of Doreen and Edmund (Lillian's son and therefore a cousin of Bunty). Doreen was idealized by Ruby and her sisters and remembered as "Auntie Doreen" (146, 236). She was the woman George had a long affair with (and whom Bunty referred to as "the Floozy"), but she took care of the girls during a fondly remembered beach holiday. Doreen becomes a fairy tale–like good mother for Ruby, Patricia, and Gillian, but she had also given up her daughter (Tessa). Ruby does not remark on the connection—it is left for the reader to see. Patricia also gave up a child when she was a teenager, and after Bunty's funeral, Patricia leaves York to search for the child she had surrendered to adoption. Patricia, like Ruby, is also investigating family history, but her interest is genealogy (332). So the integration of characters and narratives continues through the last pages of the novel.

The last pages of *Behind the Scenes at the Museum* stimulates speculation about whether the book was autobiographical. Ruby grew up a shopkeeper's daughter in York (after the pet shop fire, George opens a surgical supply shop); she attended Queen Anne's school, worked as a hotel chambermaid, becomes a single mother with two children, lives in Scotland, and is a writer: "any day now I intend to begin work on a grand project—a cycle of poems based on the family tree. There will be room for everyone . . . and who is to say which of these is real and which fiction?" (332). (Ruby's reference to a future text, "*Ruby 2-The Sequel, What Ruby Did Next!*" (314), has perhaps also fueled speculation about a sequel to the novel.) Atkinson, though, has always been aggressive in her denial of autobiographical content in her work: "When you start writing, it's for therapy—every writer has to get all that autobiographical crap out" (Aitkenhead 1996), and the same sentiments recur elsewhere. Still, Atkinson is not above playing with our speculations. Ruby imagines what she calls the "Lost Property Cupboard theory of life" (281) and of the afterlife—"where all the things we have ever lost have been kept for us-every hairgrip, every button and pencil. . . . All the library books, all the cats that never came back. . . . And perhaps, too, the other less tangible things-tempers and patience (perhaps Patricia's virginity will be there), religion (Kathleen has lost hers), meaning, innocence (mine) and oceans of time" (282). It is an image that recurs late in the book (330) and most movingly at the end of the "Wisdom" chapter: "now I know what I would put in my bottom drawer. I would put my sisters" (295). For Patricia the past is what you leave behind, but for Ruby it is what you take with you (331). The lost property cupboard is an archive of the past, but it is also a metaphor for the text itself where all the lost people and things are gathered. But the image of the locked cupboard containing the things of the past that affect the present recalls a similar object in Graham Swift's *Waterland,* which is a locked chest: "once I dabbled in history. . . . But it never got serious—my studies never began in earnest—until one August afternoon a prisoner myself of irreversibly historical events, I unlocked the past inside a black wooden chest" (276). Evoking the story of Pandora here (which Atkinson alludes to numerous times in *Started Early, Took My Dog*), Swift's narrator, Tom Crick, discovers eleven bottles—one is empty—of Coronation Ale, an extremely potent beer brewed for the coronation celebrations of George V in June 1911. The surprising thing for us is that the brewery that produced the beer is the Atkinson brewery, and every bottle is embossed "Atkinson-Gildsey." Like Jeanette Winterson, Angela Carter, and, of course, Kate Atkinson, Graham Swift reworks fairy-tale narratives in *Waterland.* The fact that the past that Crick's family narrative hinges on is the story of Atkinson's is surely interesting in light of Kate Atkinson's own work, although, of course, Swift's Atkinson family is his invention while the coincidence of names allows Kate Atkinson, through Ruby's theory of the Lost Property Cupboard to have a bit of fun. In a kind of postscript for the novel written more than a decade later, Atkinson wrote:

> The book is a repository for the past, for mine, for other people's, for the city's, a place of safekeeping for the fragile. (The Lost Property Cupboard of the book is a deeply held belief of mine. Everything Will Be Returned at the End.) The book saves things that might otherwise be lost. . . .
>
> I am not Ruby Lennox, but she is me. Her story isn't mine but the book is, in its own way, my own museum. The beginning of the book is a nod to *Tristram Shandy* (Sterne wrote it in York, the first copies were sold in Stonegate), and here I am, Shandy-wise, more or less back where I started, having never really gone anywhere. And, of course, it's not about York, or things or museums; like *Tristram Shandy,* like all literature, it's about the journey of the self towards the light. ("Night in the Museum: Kate Atkinson on the Origins," 2008)

Although a first novel, *Behind the Scenes at the Museum* interestingly looks ahead to Atkinson's later books in that the early material is reworked and developed. The sisterly rivalry between Nell and Lillian for Jack's attention looks ahead to a sisterly rivalry in *Abandonment;* Ruby's retreat to an island "where the birds outnumber the people" (332) and her work as a translator and writer anticipates Effie's and Nora's circumstances in *Emotionally Weird;* and Ruby's claim to have "been to the end of the world. I know what happens" (331) finds an echo in the short story collection *Not the End of the World* and in Isobel's narrating boasts in *Human Croquet:* "I am the alpha and omega of narrators (I am omniscient) and I know the beginning and the end" (20). We also see in the account of Edmund's death when his Halifax bomber is shot down a passage that could easily fit into *A God in Ruins* (Edward Todd has a Canadian navigator named Donald McLintock, called "Mac"; Edmund is a Canadian bomb-aimer who bails out of the burning plane with a rear-gunner, Mac McKendrick, a Scot); Patricia becomes a Buddhist, like Sunny in *A God in Ruins*, whose sister Bertie has twins. Similarly, material from earlier work is echoed in *Behind the Scenes at the Museum:* in the early short story "Karmic Mothers—Fact or Fiction?," a young girl, Agnes, imagines "her real mother had been one of the ones who dropped garnet red blood on to linen-white snow and picked up a shiny jet-black raven feathers and wished her heart out for the perfect baby girl—" (161). Ruby, in a few places, refers to herself as "a drop of blood" (43, 113, 333), but more explicitly we find, "I've been given the wrong mother and am in danger of embarking on the wrong life but I trust it will all be sorted out and I will be reunited with my real mother—the one who dropped ruby-red blood onto a snow-white handkerchief and wished for a little girl with hair the colour of a shiny jet-black raven's wing" (43). As McDermott, Tolan, and Parker all note, the evocation of the Grimm Brothers' tale of Rose Red and Snow White maps on to the Ruby/Pearl dichotomy, with Pearl remaining pure and untainted—"Pearl likes to laugh, she is all light and sunshine to my dark brooding"(291)—while Ruby is the difficult and bloody sister (Tolan 2009, 285). The fantasy of the child who is switched at birth, the "cuckoo fantasy" (McDermott 2006, 70), recurs in Atkinson's work where replacement mothers such as Auntie Doreen, Joanna Hunter in *When Will There Be Good News?,* or Tracy Waterhouse in *Started Early, Took My Dog* emerge, and in "Karmic Mothers" the notion is given literal expression in Agnes's last actions before leaving the hospital (162–63). Atkinson never repeats herself, but her body of work is clearly organic.

Human Croquet

In 2001, Atkinson considered *Human Croquet* her darkest but also the best of the three novels she had published to that point (Clark 2001). It is a departure from *Behind the Scenes at the Museum,* but it also continues narrative practices that are found in much of her work. As is the case with *Behind the Scenes at the Museum* and *Emotionally Weird, Human Croquet* is narrated by a young woman trying to understand her present and herself. And, as in *Behind the Scenes at the Museum, Human Croquet* is shaped by trauma stemming from the death of a family member; in this case, Isobel Fairfax's mother disappears, and her absence is at the narrative's core. The story anticipates, to a slightly lesser extent, the metafictional play of *Emotionally Weird,* and it works with fairy tales, Shakespeare's plays, and Ovid's *Metamorphoses,* among other intertextual layers.[9]

Isobel opens her account in the present on April 1, her sixteenth birthday—"the traditional age for spindles to start pricking and suitors to come calling and a host of other symbolic sexual imagery to suddenly manifest itself" (24), which alerts us to the importance of fairy tales—but we might soon wonder if what we are reading isn't some kind of April Fool's joke (Sanders 2001, 67), for Isobel describes herself experiencing odd things. Late in the novel we read that she has been in a coma for more than three weeks (she wakes on April 23—Shakespeare's death and his traditionally ascribed birth date) after a tree fell on her on her birthday (313–15). Consequently, the veracity of everything we've read is doubtful because it may all just be the dreaming imaginings of the unconscious girl. As the novel notes in many places, "appearances can be very deceptive" (319, similarly 198, 238, and elsewhere), and the particular account we read is, perhaps, just one version of reality. The fact is, *Human Croquet* presents multiple challenges to readers looking for verisimilitude in a straightforward family romance. Of course, we do have a rapid history of the family presented, and we have the history of the area, including the house "Arden," built after the First World War on the foundations of Fairfax Manor (19). There are some obvious historical markers in the text, most notably the Second World War, that present the story's world as "real." On the other hand, this is also a literary book that clearly identifies itself with other fictions from its opening words: "Call me Isobel" (11) evokes Melville's classic, but the passage moves on to Genesis and then to *King Lear* in rapid succession. Her slightly later play with the sound of her name, "IS-O-BEL. A PEAL OF PELLS. ISABELLA TARANTELLA—A MAD DANCE. I am mad, therefore I am. Mad. Am I? Belle, Bella, Best, never let it rest" (23), establishes language itself as a field of play. The playful "Mad. Am I?" (also a palindrome for "I'm Adam") is echoed elsewhere in the text and later tied to *Alice in Wonderland:* "We are both as mad as tea-party hatters" (77). In Isobel's account, dreams become real, time slips into the past, days are repeated with variations, and magical transformations take place.

For Atkinson, *Human Croquet* is about the imagination, while *Behind the Scenes at the Museum* is about the York of her childhood, and *Emotionally Weird* about "words and language and writing," but each is "based on *Alice in Wonderland* in one way or another" (Bunce 2000). *Human Croquet* becomes a narrative game in which the characters act out alternative destinies while participating in a particular historical moment. We cannot really prioritize any single narrative path, although we may prefer one to another. For example, which ending for Baxter, an abusive neighbor who murders Eliza, would we like to see? Is he a suicide by gunshot (315); stabbed by his wife with a carving knife, as in Conrad's *The Secret Agent* (257–58); or poisoned by her before she shoots him (318)? Fiction provides "real right justice" (319), so perhaps it is enough to know he is dead. Did Audrey, Baxter's daughter and Isobel's friend, have a baby? Or did she miscarry (316)? Which, if any, Christmas Eve is actually experienced? Surely, one of them is "wish fulfillment" (275), as Isobel acknowledges, but none actually "happens" if Isobel's stay in the hospital in April 1960 is the "truth." When she wakes there, like Alice "finding she dreamt the looking-glass world," Isobel feels "cheated" by her imagination, "unconfined by cause and effect. But then how else can we make things work out right?" (319).

The novel is a fictional construct made out of words, many of which are identified with other textual constructs. It is telling that Isobel so often draws attention to the sense of words, particularly those employed in idiomatic expressions or clichés: "If you spend time what do you buy? 'Less time,' Mrs Baxter says sadly" (53); or elsewhere, "'and if you can find time, read ahead to the next chapter of your textbook.' Find time? Where might it be located? In space? . . . If we found time would it solve all our problems?" (125–26). Chapters alternate between sections labeled "Present" and "Past," and toward the end of the book, we have "Future," but then we also have a section called, "Maybe," which not only acknowledges that some things are uncertain but also that other narrative paths, other timelines are possible. Time does, indeed, move on (187), and after seven years, Isobel and Charles's father, Gordon, who had disappeared, returns with Debbie, a stepmother. His appearance is signaled by the repetition of Gordon's sister Vinny's "There's somebody at the back door." To which Isobel replies, "'I didn't hear anyone.' . . . 'That doesn't mean there isn't someone there,' Vinny said" (184–85). The phrasing is formulaic, almost identical to earlier occurrences. On the first occasion, Isobel finds a dog at the door (66); on the second, she finds a baby (135). Each moment represents a narrative possibility that unfolds.

Isobel seems to float in time. Indeed, not only does the description of her birth locate her in the twentieth century but a reference to the "second-best bedroom in Arden" also links her to Shakespeare's time while the scent of spring ties her to the seasonal cycle: "And so Isobel was born on the street of trees, near the muddled middle of the twentieth century, in a country at war, on the lumpy feather mattress of the second-best bedroom in Arden, her very first breath scented with the sour sappiness of new hawthorn" (90).[10] Isobel also finds herself suddenly transported in time while she remains in the same space but in now a different era: "Why am I dropping into random pockets of time and then popping back out again? Am I really doing it or am I imagining that I'm doing it? Is this some kind of epistemological ordeal I've been set? I should never have tried to kill time. I wasted it and now its wasting me [paraphrasing *Richard II*]. If I had more control it might be useful—" (143). Later, her repeated Christmas Eve experiences cause her to ponder the matter again, "Can you step in the same river *thrice*" (271), which evokes Heraclitus for the third time as well (earlier on 243 and then on 251). Within the realm of the text, time's arrow is bent (253) and we do move from "present" to "past" and back again, but the text is an imagined construct and "only the imagination can embrace the impossible—the golden mountain, the fire-breathing dragon, the happy ending" (323). This line suitably appears just at the end of a brief section describing her sexual encounter with Shakespeare, who "tastes of cloves" (323). Shakespeare, through his work, has been present on so many levels—Isobel, at this point, is watching an amateur performance of *Midsummer Night's Dream* from her bedroom window—that the literal appearance of the man should hardly be surprising, yet this moment does occur after she wakes from her coma and is, in fact, the end of the "present" section. As Kevin Paul Smith notes, this would place the narrative in the category of Todorov's "uncanny": its marvelous aspects escaping the containment of realism (2007, 74). Isobel's experience with time, we will see, looks ahead to *Life After Life* where Ursula Todd experiences repeated births and fractally varied lives.

Yet, the marvelous does not invalidate *Human Croquet*'s thematic concerns or the importance we accord the trauma narrative that, as in *Behind the Scenes at the Museum,* is central. In the case of *Human Croquet,* Isobel declares the "Absence of Eliza has shaped our lives" (27). For Isobel and her brother, Charles, who developed a keen interest in mysterious disappearances and alien abductions, their mother, Eliza, is only present in a few scattered found objects (a shoe, a compact) and for Isobel perhaps too in the odor of melancholy that she perceives (24). As in *Behind the Scenes at the Museum,* innocuous objects are the tangible signs that people and events in fading memory, story, and historical accounts actually possessed palpable being. Isobel and Charles are both children, seven and nine years of age, when their mother and, soon after, their father disappeared, leaving them in the care of Vinny and, until she dies in a fall, their grandmother Charlotte, who is known as the "Widow" in Isobel's account. Eliza's disappearance is never explained to them except in the cruel terms provided by their aunt and grandmother: "'Your mummy isn't coming home. She's gone away.' 'Gone away? Where?' Charles shouted, . . . 'Calm down, Charles,' the Widow said. 'She was never what you'd call very *reliable.*' Unreliable? This hardly seemed an adequate explanation of Eliza's disappearance. 'I don't believe you, you're lying!' Charles yelled at her. 'She wouldn't leave us!' 'Well, she has, I'm afraid, Charles,' the Widow said dispassionately" (159–60). Viciously, Vinny later suggests Eliza left because the children were so naughty (163). Of course, the Widow and Vinny are lying about Eliza, and they lie about the children's father too, telling them he is dead (161). That lie is exposed when he returns after a seven-year absence with his new wife, Debbie. What is telling about the story of Eliza's leaving is that the children are right to doubt it, for in an earlier section, "Half-Day Closing," which is richly evocative of "Babes in the Woods" and "Hansel and Gretel," the children come upon the body of their mother propped against a tree. They don't acknowledge she is dead and so bury her in leaves to protect her; then they search for their father and aunt (117–19). In fact, Eliza's death is repressed by the children, although the adverbial "gravely" (159) puns to reveal that repressed knowledge. Vinny and the Widow have always been hostile toward Eliza, and now with their ascension in the children's lives, they are placed in the role of the "wicked stepmother" (before an actual stepmother appears), the moral contrast to the idealized "good" mother that fairy tales so often use.

As Kevin Paul Smith points out, adaptations of fairy tales have proved fertile ground for many contemporary writers. Angela Carter, Jeanette Winterson, and Graham Swift, to name a few, have used fairy tales to contrast times and circumstances. Julie Sanders suggests Atkinson "is especially interested in the fairy tale's invocation of the family both as an ideal and as an entity capable of horrific dysfunctionality" (2006, 87), and certainly the "Half-Day Closing" chapter is explicit in this regard because Isobel notes that the casual observer would think them "a nice family—healthy, attractive, ordinary—the kind that graced the advertisements every week in *Picture Post*" (111). This appearance is deceptive, and shortly thereafter we find the children alone and in the woods after finding their mother's body: "Their only blueprint for survival in these circumstances, it seemed, was fictional. They knew the plot unfortunately, and any minute expected to find the gingerbread cottage—and then the nightmare would really begin" (117). The contrast here is underscored later in the novel when Isobel ponders the differences between stories Mrs. Baxter tells, such as "Little Red Riding Hood," and those Isobel learned from Eliza: "Mrs Baxter knew the same stories as Eliza but when Eliza had told them they had frequently ended badly and contained a great deal of mutilation and torture, whereas in Mrs Baxter's versions, the stories all had happy endings" (173). Mrs. Baxter is Isobel's fairy godmother, even making, as in "Cinderella," Isobel's dress for the Christmas Eve party she attends. The contrast between competing versions of familiar tales is striking, hence the sense of nightmarish foreboding the children feel in the woods. For Atkinson,

> Fairy stories teach girls about life. They teach girls about how to negotiate the pitfalls of living in a male world . . . They're all about girls. . . . They are also about property and economy. Because if you are living in a time when women die a lot, then you are always going to have stepmothers; you're going to have property divided up; you're going to have the girls sent away. So in a way, fairy tales have a lot to do with primogenecy: who gets the money, who gets the property, who gets the father's love. . . . But they are to do with girls." (Tolan 2008, 8–9)

She makes similar points elsewhere (Jackson 2009); indeed, in *A God in Ruins,* Edward Todd's wife, Nancy, likens fairy tales to Girl Guide handbooks (302).

As is the case in *Behind the Scenes at the Museum,* the family structure in *Human Croquet* is fraught with conflict even before Eliza's disappearance and after. Indeed, in Isobel's history of the Fairfaxes, we learn that brutality, incest, and a vanished wife—elements found in many fairy tales—are the legacy of Sir Francis Fairfax, whose house and family are imagined as cursed. In Isobel's "present," however, brutality and incest are the province of Mr. Baxter, although the decline of the Fairfax family fortune is theirs alone.

Eliza, who shares the name of Ruby's wild aunt (and anticipates Renee Miller in *Life After Life* in a way that is similar to Baxter's anticipation of Derek Oliphant also in *Life After Life,* and of other abusers in Atkinson's fiction), is of uncertain origin, thought to be the kidnapped child, Esme, of rich adoptive parents, Sir Edward de Breville and Lady Irene, an Argentinean cattle heiress (286). Eliza was raised as Violet Angela by Harold and Maude Potter, the latter of whom, bereft over her own series of miscarriages and the recent stillbirth of a girl, walks off with a baby left in an unattended pram. Violet Angela grows to be a difficult child and the victim of sexual abuse by Harold and then by a neighbor, Mr. Reagan. Promiscuous and uncontrollable, she runs off at sixteen and is soon working as a prostitute for Dickie Landers, who gives her the name Eliza Jane Dennis (301) and, in Pygmalion fashion, shapes her behavior (302). Dickie is fortuitously killed in the Blitz (Eliza had been wondering how to break from him), but Eliza survives and is found by Gordon: "My hero" (84, 218, 305). The final detail in this complicated narrative is that Sir Edward de Breville had purchased Eliza as an infant from the Paris streets (310) because his wife could not have children. A consequence of this information is that Eliza's cuckoo fantasy, "I must have been stolen from my real parents" (297), is in fact true, while the text's earlier suggestion that an unknowing Eliza had sex with her birth father (303) is dismissed, although the sordid nature of Eliza's childhood and adolescence renders the point moot. The whole sad tale of Eliza then seems to depend on her mysterious origins which, it is hinted, account for her sexually precocious behavior that ultimately leads her to her affair with the brutally abusive Baxter.

On the other hand, Eliza is clearly a victim of patriarchy and mistreatment at the hands of the men she encounters who, since her infancy, have exchanged her for money. That she uses men to satisfy her material desires renders her an object of scorn by Vinny and the Widow (e.g., 87, 104). Yet, for her children, Eliza is a loving mother, and her disappearance makes her an increasingly idealized figure in their imaginations. Stepmother Debbie, by contrast, is presented as increasingly delusional and ineffective while Mrs. Baxter is idealized. As in *Behind the Scenes at the Museum,* and in many fairy tales, good mothers and bad mothers are contrasted, but in Atkinson the distinction is always qualified (as it was in the case of Doreen, who was idealized by the Lennox girls but who gave up her own child). In *Human Croquet,* Debbie is delusional in one strand of the book's narration but in another is the person who saves Isobel's life. In that latter strand, Debbie has her own baby, but in the former she takes the foundling for her own. The Cinderella story, like other fairy tales, echoes everywhere in the novel. When Gordon finds Eliza emerging from the bombed house, she is missing a shoe, which he goes to retrieve. Charles later finds another missing shoe before he comes upon the body of Eliza (years later he finds that shoe in the back of a wardrobe). Isobel is identified with Cinderella earlier too: next to the Walshes, Hilary and Dorothy, "I'm a chimney-sweep, a walnut-skinned beggar girl" (41). Kevin Paul Smith develops this and other connections in his book.

References to fairy tales, Shakespeare, and other texts abound in *Human Croquet,* especially as Isobel, who is studying English literature, narrates some of the later parts of her history (hence, Malcolm Lovat's mother is described as looking "a bit like a character from Beckett" [195]). The same situation obtains in *Emotionally Weird,* where Effie is studying literature but allusiveness is a feature of all of Atkinson's work. As Emma Parker points out, Atkinson's use of allusion helps break down canonical hierarchies, but it also reminds us that narratives are made out of other narratives or out of what Roland Barthes calls "the already read" (*déjà-lu*) (1974, 19–20). Indeed, any narrative is constituted according to a series of codes involving the conventions of grammar, genre, and narration as well as typology, allusion, and quotation. This conception of the text as an intertextual web—as Bakhtin, Kristeva, and Barthes, among others, observe—drastically reduces the role of the author;[11] subject to discursive forces, the text constructs itself almost without the controlling presence of the author. In *Human Croquet,* Shakespeare's actual presence as a person is surely intended to remind us that "Shakespeare" the work, while culturally venerated, is the product of a human being. Shakespeare's plays are an obvious point of reference for Isobel, who lives in a house named Arden and is writing an essay on "*Twelfth Night*—'Appearances can be deceptive: discuss'" (203).

Ovid's *Metamorphoses* also plays an important role in *Human Croquet,* most explicitly when Isobel undergoes a transformation similar to Daphne's when she is threatened with sexual assault at a Christmas party (239). Earlier, however, Isobel had translated part of Ovid's text, the story of Phaeton's sisters (significantly, given her family circumstances, an account of grief) for school (146–47), and the chapter, "The Art of Successful Entertaining" opens with her waking from a "Bizarre Ovidian dream" (230). ("Phaeton's sisters" are referred at the outset of the novel as well [12].) At the party, in one telling, Isobel is chased by a group of teenaged boys, who have been fed lies about Isobel's sexual availability, into the backyard and she is trapped. Her plea, "Why do I have no protector in this world, someone watching over me?" (239), echoes Daphne's prayer (Sanders 2001, 78) and reminds us of her mother's absence, but Isobel then discovers that she has been transformed into a birch tree, rendering her invisible to her pursuers; one even leans against the tree. Returning to the house, she reflects in a way that recalls the book's opening, "I am not what I am. I am a tree therefore

I am mad, a mad person subject to massive delusions and hallucinations" (239). There is no explanation for how these things could happen, and, indeed, this is only part of the first accounting of the same Christmas Eve, which is then repeated with variations.

Isobel's Ovidian escape is clearly fantastical and may recall similar escapes beyond Ovid's telling, such as Fevver's in Angela Carter's *Nights at the Circus:* when threatened with captivity by a Russian grand duke, Fevvers leaps on to a train that had a moment before been a toy dropped on a rug, "mercifully, it landed on its wheels" (192), and she escapes into Siberia. As was the case with Carter, who was an obvious influence on her (Sanders 2010, 88), Atkinson was regarded by some reviewers as a "magic realist" after *Human Croquet* appeared, but she had little sympathy for those who sought to label her work: "People talk about magic realism and fantasy all the time. I don't know what magic realism is. A novel isn't real: a novel is fiction, it's fantasy. So why is some realism more real than others?" (Tolan 2008, 5). Elsewhere she remarked, "I don't like being put in a genre, . . . [people] can label me if they want, as long as I don't label myself" (Butki 2011). And in *Emotionally Weird,* she appears to mock the very idea of magic realism in Nora's misguided use of the term: "—So is that magic realism? Nora asks. 'No, it's fiction'" (205; later Effie will demonstrate what she calls "magic realism" [330]).

Links among "magic realism," "metafiction," and postmodernism are tangled, and critical discussion has evolved over the last number of decades to articulate distinctions, but it is postmodernism's aesthetic that is near to Atkinson's thinking.[12] *Human Croquet*'s tale of traumatic loss is filtered through a literary sensibility that works with narratives of a once aristocratic family's decline and a young person's coming of age. The story of the Fairfax family and its demise, the seeds of which Isobel finds in a prosperous origin, is important to Isobel's understanding of her place in the modern world. The very distant past—in Isobel's account, biblical creation and evolutionary development following the big bang—is evoked to situate the present era within an extended continuity of time and space. Isobel's unbidden visits to the past demonstrate persistent change that, erasing the world she knows, leaves only language in its place. Spaces gain the names of absent things as forest gives way to houses: "Different trees for every street-Ash Street, Chestnut Avenue, . . . The forest of trees had become a wilderness of streets" (19). Words become the means by which one can make sense of one's origins, identity, and place in the world and history. But words are separate from those named things, and, as Isobel often says, they are frequently open to question (as Isobel often does). So if language builds a world, what is the status of that world when language slips its moorings? The problem extends to identity. Isobel often ponders the meaning of common expressions, dead metaphors, and the notion of self: "I'm not myself" (109),

Eliza mutters, and of Audrey, Isobel remarks, "'She's not herself,' I say vaguely (but then who is?)" (125). The existence of "The real me. The true self" (71) is implied in the utterances of many of the book's characters (Audrey, Malcolm, Eliza, Isobel, for example), but tellingly their pervasive commentary suggests an authentic self is recessive, always just somewhere else, ultimately perhaps an illusory imago. Poststructuralist psychoanalytic theory developed by Jacques Lacan and Julia Kristeva has dealt with this problem. Lacan posits the formation of a sense of self occurring in the mirror stage when the preverbal child recognizes itself as if looking in a mirror as the "Ideal-I": "this form situates the agency of the ego, before its social determination, in a fictional direction, which will always remain irreducible for the individual alone" (1977, 2). Later the self identifies itself as an other shaped by the codings of the symbolic realm, yet the self as one experiences it, as one feels oneself to be, is constantly shaped in the act of narration in ways that render it subject to forces that fail to produce a comparable sense of the self as it is experienced and lived. The "Ideal-I," in its wholeness, appears contrary to the self's own awareness of itself as a fragmented and conflicted entity. Later, when the self is constituted in language, this gap between the imaginary and the symbolic self persists. The "I" is outside its own statements about itself, yet these statements are the only means by which the "I" can represent itself to itself. The self, then, is always already an other signifying not an absence but a pretext lying outside of consciousness's conceiving of itself and beyond articulation.

"Appearances can be deceptive" (238), we are often told in *Human Croquet,* so the self we see is an unstable entity, not a fixed thing but "in process/on trial" (Kristeva 1986, 91). The narrative of events, too, is unstable as multiple versions and possibilities are offered—all of which take us if not to *the* ending at least to *endings:* the cosmic apocalypse, a piece of a poem "Thomas the Rhymer," a description of "human croquet" (complete with an illustration!) from *The Home Entertainer* (first published in the 1920s), and finally, a simple, perhaps apocalyptic "END" alone on the page, just as "PRESENT," "PAST," and "FUTURE" appeared earlier. Atkinson does provide a kind of ending for Isobel's narrative in a way that is similar to *Behind the Scenes at the Museum*'s last section in that we read of the mature Isobel's current circumstances and the fates of her friends, Carmen and Eunice; Malcolm; her brother Charles; her aunt Vinny; her younger half-sister, Renee; and Hilary Walsh, who is now a friend. We also learn she has a grown daughter, Imogen, and, perhaps most telling, that she is a successful writer of historical romances, which casts light on those sections in the novel dealing with Sir Francis and Lady Fairfax. Certainly, the "Original Sin" (327–34) chapter is very much a self-contained piece that incorporates many of the motifs (abuse, adultery, incest) that are part of Isobel's larger narrative of her adolescent life and childhood. Is she, as a writer of fiction, drawing on elements of her past, or is the short story "Original Sin" another fiction, another variant in the textual field that is *Human Croquet*? Certainly on one level, "Original Sin," as its title suggests, is the source of family catastrophe, but only if we take the notion of a curse as credible. The many narrative connections between the sixteenth-century Fairfax past and the present occur on multiple levels, and Shakespeare as both the person and the work bridges the centuries. Sir Francis's brutality is echoed in Baxter's, as is his incestuous relations with his daughter.[13] Audrey carries the weight of that plot in the present, but Isobel does speculate on the idea of incest and at one point suggests, "Perhaps incest wouldn't be so bad if it was with someone you were so close to. Malcolm Lovat, for example" (203). The irony here is that Malcolm is Isobel's half-brother because he is the baby Eliza gave up before she married Gordon (301).

The incestuous ties that are hinted at or perhaps occur point to the way narratives in *Human Croquet* become tangled with each other, with, say, one detail altering the course of an imagined path. For instance, the "discovery" that Eliza was found—"purchased"—on the Paris streets suggests she avoided incest with her father. Similarly, the multiple accounts of Christmas Eve vary because some things, such as the fire at the party that kills Hilary and her brother, Richard, for example, do not happen. All these Christmas accounts, however, end with the trauma of Malcolm Lovat's death—something Isobel, aware of what will happen, tries on the last occasion to prevent (277). But, as in *Life After Life,* we are spared the full impact of this catastrophe because he returns, and in the final pages we learn that he has survived the narrative to die in squalor, a casualty of drink and drugs in the late 1960s (339). The discovery of a baby on the doorstep is also replayed for us, but we cannot finally tell if it is Audrey's child or not. Did Audrey give birth? Did she miscarry? Was she even pregnant? Even Eliza's murder is never really solved (or even investigated). Gordon confesses to Isobel (214) but later retracts his claim with the qualifying: "I killed her spirit" (229); in the account of her death told later from Eliza's perspective, someone named Peter is responsible, although description tells us he is Baxter.

Can all of these things be true? The answer is nowhere except in the imagination where everything is possible (323). Does Isobel control her movement through time or is her existence at any moment the haphazard result of a particular carom in molecular activity? Can she step in the same river twice or even thrice? The multiple Christmas Eves she experiences all end the same way, but in the last one she lies in the wreck and feels "a pair of warm lips cover my own icy ones" (278). As her thoughts drift she feels ecstatic, a once hapless girl transformed into "something rich and strange. . . . I am as full of ecstasy as an archangel—I am my true self" (279). The moment does not last and she wakes in "the fearful place, the heart of the heart of the forest." In these last pages of the chapter, "There Is Another World But It Is This One," Isobel's jumbled thoughts resolve into her waking in hospital listening to a "strange and hypnotic" voice: "After days, possibly weeks, maybe years, I realize that she's telling me a story. She is my own Scheherazade, she knows everything, she must be the storyteller from the end of the world. But how does it begin? Why it begins, as it must, she says, with the arrival of the baby—" (282). It isn't clear who this other patient Isobel knows from somewhere might be, but the description reminds us of the novel's opening: "I am Isobel Fairfax, I am the alpha and omega of narrators (I am omniscient) and I know the beginning and the end. . . . And in between are all the stories" (20). Isobel is her own Scheherazade, and she has awakened at the point of origin in the telling—the baby. For readers, "the baby" in the next few pages is Esme (later Eliza), but on another level it is the mysterious baby found at the door, and on yet another it is Isobel born on in the "second-best bedroom" out of a Platonic world of forms where she was her true self. The baby is a beginning, an origin, but which path will it follow? Any path is a story, fractally separating from a point of origin—the noise at the door is a strange dog (66) or a foundling (136): "(Isn't this the way the Dog was introduced into the story? I must be having a *déjà vu,* one more alarming little snag in the fabric of time, I suppose)" (135–36).[14] The narrative swells in a four-dimensional web, and words, which must run linearly, cannot follow these many paths except through the connotative worlds of metaphor and allusion. Isobel is Alice in her own wonderland (319), "confused by the different versions of reality. The Dog, for example, is delighted to see me and is virtually the same Dog as before, but not quite (doG perhaps). . . . And the Lythe Players' production of *A Midsummer Night's Dream* is due to take place as before, but Debbie for some reason is now playing Hermia rather than Helena, only a few letters different and much the same plot function, but nonetheless mystifying" (319). Anything is possible in the imagination's fluid realm, but the book must have an ending: "I am the storyteller at the end of time. I know how it ends. It ends like this" (343), with a period. And yet pages remain—"Thomas the Rhymer," "A Good Game for a Party," an illustration—finally, after a blank page, "END" (351), and that's it.

Emotionally Weird

Toward the end of *Behind the Scenes at the Museum,* Ruby Lennox says, "The past's what you take with you" (331). While her observation resonates on many levels in that novel, it also speaks to Atkinson's growth, for motifs, themes, and structures are developed across all her books: family dynamics, particularly relationships between mothers and daughters, and a concern with history, with Englishness, and with storytelling itself are always foregrounded. We also find highly allusive, often playful language and a fondness for parallel narratives, frequently crossing different historical moments. In *Behind the Scenes at the Museum,* as we saw, Ruby's narrative is interrupted by "Footnotes" recounting matrilineal family history that echoes through time, gesture, and genetic inheritance: as Bunty says to Ruby as they gaze at the photo of Alice and her children, "'She [Alice] looks just like you'" (29). These "footnotes" are not the stories generally preserved in memory, so it is Ruby's task to tell them. Isobel Fairfax in *Human Croquet* similarly imagines an ancestral past that, while structured along fairy tale and romance narratives, nonetheless informs her present moment.

The idea of multiple narrative strands existing in the same frame is everywhere in Atkinson's work, from *Abandonment*'s double-sidedness to *Case Histories* several cases to *Life After Life*'s numerous recountings with differences of Ursula Todd's many lives. Similarly, the linkages between *A God in Ruins* and *Life After Life* again point to Atkinson's enjoyment in developing twined narrative strands. Nothing is ever lost: dogs and character types self-consciously recur in the books, while historical material—the Second World War, for instance—reemerges as central. Edward Todd's experiences in the Royal Air Force in *A God in Ruins* have a textual precursor in Atkinson's first novel when Ruby's cousin Edmund is shot down: Atkinson's own work is also part of the archive of material that she draws on. In *Human Croquet,* for example, Isobel's friend Eunice lists various fears: "'Gephyrophobia—fear of bridges.' 'Right,' I say vaguely. 'Dromophobia—fear of crossing the street? Potamophobia—fear of rivers? Perhaps,' Eunice says airily, 'some deep-seated terror in your past is coming back to revisit you'" (71–72).[15] Isobel has much to be terrified about, of course, but the scene recalls a moment from *Behind the Scenes at the Museum* when Patricia and Ruby watch some swans from a bridge over an icy river—it is a time when Ruby seems closest to the memory of Pearl's death: "'they have each other,' I add. . . . A shiver goes through me from top to bottom. 'The water looks so *cold*'" (204). Similarly, Effie (Euphemia), the narrator in *Emotionally Weird,* is named "for Nora's sister, [Nora is Effie's ostensible mother] who drowned in a river on the day that I was born" (21). In *Behind the Scenes at the Museum,* Ruby names one of her daughters for her drowned sister, Pearl.

Emotionally Weird proved difficult for Atkinson to write; its composition laborious (Bunce 2000). She later recounted, "I wasn't well, and I had no joy in writing anymore. The stories [*Not the End of the World*] re-established the joy in writing" (Tolan 2008, 10). None of her struggles come across in the book, which is very funny. Like its predecessors, its main character and narrator is a young woman, Effie, telling Nora, whom Effie believes is her mother, about life at Dundee University, her classes, friends, and schoolwork, while Nora talks about her life and family, which naturally includes details about Effie's life. The family history that emerges from their overlapping tales is only fully discernable late in the book, but the veracity of their histories is open to question. As *Emotionally Weird* opens, Effie and Nora are on a deserted island off the coast of

Scotland (recalling the place where the adult Ruby Lennox settled to work as a translator and poet) that was the vacation home of Nora's once prosperous family, the Stuart-Murrays. Because of poor weather, they are isolated and use the stories to entertain themselves. The book opens, however, with a draft of Effie's creative writing assignment, which is a detective story called "The Hand of Fate," featuring Madame Astarti as a seaside tarot reader and amateur sleuth. Pieces of that story follow at various points, although it is not completed until much later in the course of the book. What ensues in the novel, among other things, is a discussion heavily marked by postmodernist theory related to mimesis in fiction and, to a lesser extent, an academic discussion of detective fiction. As Atkinson notes in her introduction to a Penguin reissue of Robert Coover's story collection *Pricksongs and Descants,* Coover and other American writers in the 1960s "were eager to move away from what [John] Barth called the 'literature of exhaustion' . . . towards a new aesthetic for fiction where the pretense of 'reality' was abandoned, along with an attempt at extracting 'meaning.' . . . The restraints of narrative convention were discarded, to be replaced with self-aware, self-absorbed texts that ran riot with linguistic acrobatics and an insistence on the medium rather than the message. The fictive process itself was the thing" (*v–vi*). *Human Croquet* flouts mimesis in many places—indeed, the whole account may well be a dream—and mimesis is similarly defied in *Emotionally Weird* when, again, scenes repeat themselves with difference. The academic discussion in *Emotionally Weird,* of course, not only demonstrates Atkinson's familiarity with the discipline and literary theory (gained from her own student days) but will echo, less obviously, in future novels. She certainly strikes back at those such as Hoggart, who notoriously suggested of *Behind the Scenes at the Museum* that she was postmodern without being aware of what it meant.

"Text," as Professor Archie McCue in *Emotionally Weird* reminds us in a chapter called "The Art of Structuralist Criticism," derives from the Latin, "*textum,*" meaning "web" (51), and Atkinson's fiction amply demonstrates the truth of this etymology, for it constitutes an intertextual web of narrative and allusion that touches a vast range of cultural expression from classical myth to popular songs, film, and culture as well as literature. Speaking to Fiona Tolan about her allusiveness in her first books, Atkinson said, "I think I had a lot of stuff in me that was informing my thinking and that I needed to reference. . . . Those three books are all coming from the same place, and were a lot to do with my childhood reading, my adolescent reading, my university reading: to do with literature" (Tolan 2008, 10). In *Emotionally Weird,* Atkinson is particularly adept at using allusion and cultural references to establish the milieu of undergraduate life circa 1972. Along with references to authors and texts that are perhaps more usual (Lewis Carroll, Samuel Taylor Coleridge, Edgar Allan Poe, Bertolt Brecht,

Emily Dickinson, and Laurence Sterne, for example), we see mention of authors who were popular student reading in the period (J. R. R. Tolkien, Mervyn Peake, Hermann Hesse), television (*Star Trek, Dr. Who, The Prisoner*), and music (King Crimson, CSNY, Joni Mitchell). (These are by no means exhaustive lists.)

This period matches her own student days at the University of Dundee, but *Emotionally Weird* is far from autobiographical. Atkinson, we've noted, has adamantly expressed her horror of biographical readings, and in *Emotionally Weird* several passages comment on the hazards of fiction rooted in autobiography: about one of her creative writing classmates, Effie remarks, "So far, all Andrea had written were flimsy stories about a girl called Anthea who came from Northhallerton and was studying English literature at university. . . . Anthea was always having poignant moments sparked off by mundane experiences—going to lectures, finding spiders, buying A4 narrow-ruled with margins. Personally I think that reading the details of other people's domesticity is almost as tiresome as listening to them recount their dreams" (41–42). Later, "Martha was always urging us to 'Write what you know,' (how boring books would be if everyone adhered to that principle!)" (172). The irony is that *Emotionally Weird* clearly draws on Atkinson's student experience, but the book itself constantly challenges fiction's relationship to the real, essentially arguing, as so many of Atkinson's postmodern mentors do, that the writer of fiction is free to do anything, whether plausible or not.[16] Effie and Nora often argue the point: "Plot development? Nora murmurs quietly, almost to herself. 'Is not necessary in this post-modern day and age,' I tell her firmly." (186); or, more explicitly, "'Go on, carry on with your unlikely tale.' ~ Effie grew up, eventually. Got married, got divorced (twice), died. End of story. 'You can't do that.' ~ It's the post-modern day and age. I can do what I want" (251). Consequently, any attempt to read Atkinson's life into *Emotionally Weird* or her other books falters. Of course, one's experiences and the world one knows will inform one's writing, but it is pointless to seek out those moments in her texts that relate to her life: "'They say everyone has a novel inside them, don't they?' Chick said [Chick is a private investigator who repeatedly encounters Effie and her friends], warming to his subject now. 'Yeah, and maybe that's where it should stay,' Terri growled" (93). Atkinson, it seems, would agree with Terri (which does not mean others cannot disagree and some of them can be quite successful—a final joke in *Emotionally Weird:* "And the winner of the Booker Prize for the year 2001 is . . . Andrea Garnett for her novel *Anthea's Anguish*" [411]).

Emotionally Weird exaggerates Atkinson's indulgence in allusion, word play, jokes, and fictional possibilities. As a "comic novel"—Effie's own description (365) as well as the book's subtitle—*Emotionally Weird* is lighter in tone than its predecessors. Jokes abound with something funny on almost every page. And, in keeping with the comic form, the final pages answer hanging questions. Both Effie's and Nora's narratives end happily; indeed, Nora's even includes a wedding as she marries a diver. As was the case in the earlier novels, a brief epilogue set in 1999 and beyond offers updates about several of the characters including Effie, who, we learn, is now a successful writer of cozy detective stories. Her course assignment, *The Hand of Fate,* teasingly interspersed throughout the novel, was published soon after Effie left university and became the first in a series of books: it is reissued because of a television adaptation (405). Again, one suspects an inside joke here as Effie's movement from academic writing (she struggles to write an essay on George Eliot's *Middlemarch*) to detective story writer anticipates Atkinson's turn to the genre in *Case Histories.* Which is not to say Effie is Atkinson—a fact doubly reinforced by the usual disclaimer appearing prior to the epigraph from *Through the Looking-Glass* that "Neither are any of the characters portrayed based on anyone real, either living or dead" and by the repetition of similar statement at the end of *Emotionally Weird* that is part of Effie's opening apparatus, complete with promotional blurbs, for the reissue of her *Hand of Fate* (405).

Still, the text's logic implies that everything we read here is fiction; certainly, the disclaimer on *Hand of Fate* is, so why not the prefatory warning as well? Like Alice in the looking-glass world, we are lost in *Emotionally Weird*'s hall of mirrors for the text is continually self-reflective, with storytelling itself being the book's overarching concern as Effie and Nora each comment on and critique each other's efforts in dialogue that might recall Lewis Carroll's: "~ Is any of this going anywhere? Nora asks, staring into her teacup like a fortune teller. 'Well, it's leading here, eventually. As you know.' ~ It's a rather roundabout route" (143–44). Effie's—and, to a lesser extent, Nora's—accounts dominate the book, but many of those at the university are also writers practicing in a variety of genres. Their texts, like Effie's and Nora's, are presented with distinct typefaces that allow readers to determine narrators and time frames while also, to some degree, reflecting their source and form. Excerpts from Archie McCue's *The Expanding Prism of J.* (a sly reference to William Gaddis's *JR*?) are in a tightly bolded font while excerpts from *The Wards of Love,* a romance written by his wife, Philippa, are in a neat cursive (e.g., 225 and 230). *The Hand of Fate* is double-spaced in a Courier font (to imitate a typewriter), while Kevin's fantasy tale is strikingly represented in a Gothic font. There are other writers and other typefaces in the book too; there is even, borrowing from Sterne's *Tristram Shandy,* half a page that is solidly black after a dog is hit by Chick's car (85)—Terri revives the animal, which then reappears in Effie's story. (In *Human Croquet* the greatly increased size of the font marked crucial moments, for example, "A Baby" [137].) In *Emotionally Weird,* the range of discourses employed clearly demonstrates the constructed nature of the novel as text.

The early chapter "The Art of Structuralist Criticism" can in many ways serve as a gloss on *Emotionally Weird* at large. In this scene Effie and her friends attend Archie McCue's seminar and listen, puzzled, to his lecture on contemporary literary theory (ca. 1972). The students are bewildered, but readers acquainted with the discourse will find these remarks cogent and relevant for the novel. Archie asserts, for instance, that "writers who eschew mimesis, looking for new ways of approaching the fiction construct, are disruptivist—challenging what Robbe-Grillet refers to as 'intelligibility of the world'" (39). Later, we read—but Effie misses the verb's subject as her attention has been diverted because Archie, distracted by Andrea crossing her legs, lost his train of thought—

> ". . . made by several structuralist critics that it is only at the moment that the written word in literature ceases to refer to external 'objective' data, that is to referents in the 'real' world, that it can begin to exist as a language within the text . . . What the new fiction reminds us," Archie yakked on, "is that signs need only refer to imaginary construct-that perhaps that is all they do refer to, for perhaps it's not the job of fiction to make sense of the world." (45)

Perhaps not, but Ruby Lennox clearly said otherwise in *Behind the Scenes at the Museum:* "words are the only things that can construct a world that makes sense" (332). The scene is not without its parodic qualities, however, as several people—late students, Professor Cousins (the department head, an old-fashioned Shakespearian who is fond of word games), Martha Sewell (an American creative writing instructor and poet "whom no-one in the department had ever heard of" [54]), and an unidentified other (the sequence breaks off as Nora has heard enough [60])—drop into the quickly crowded room: "'It's like Waterloo Station in here,' Prof Cousins said cheerfully. 'I don't know when you get any teaching done, Archie'" (59). While not achieving the madcap density of the Marx Brothers' "two hard-boiled eggs" scene from *A Night at the Opera,* the moment is ridiculous and the crowd stifling (58). From a narrative perspective, however, this gathering of characters allows Effie—or, rather, Atkinson—to introduce many of the book's characters, and in Effie's hands they tend to be described as "types"; that is, Martha Sewell is "an Amherst-type" (54), Andrea is "one of those girls who . . ." (44), "Martha and Jay belonged to the class of people who . . ." (55), Watson Grant (sometimes referred to as Grant Watson [242]) "was one of the no-hope challengers" (to succeed Cousins as department head) (65), even Andrea's flat is described as "one of those university places where no-one knows each other at the beginning of the year and no-one likes each other by the end" (75)—all of which tends to generalize Effie's university experience.

Amid the absurdity of the seminar scene, though, a debate about fiction does occur with Professor Cousins offering a traditionally humanist assessment of literature's purpose—"don't you think, Archie, . . . that really all literature is about the search for *identity*? . . . The *meaning* of life. And God, . . . does He—or She—exist and if so why does He—or She—leave us bereft in a cold and lonely world, spinning endlessly'" (53)—that is contrasted with the postmodern skepticism of Archie McCue that Effie parrots without understanding (59). Later in the novel a similarly parodic companion scene occurs that tends, because of its focus on Effie's and the students' bewilderment, to demonstrate the perception that contemporary theory leaves the literary text behind. Students expect a lecture on George Eliot's work, but Maggie Mackenzie never mentions Eliot, although she does mention Roland Barthes, Louis Althusser, and Sigmund Freud (229–32): "'I thought she was going to be talking about *Middlemarch,*' Andrea hissed. 'Maybe she *is* talking about it and we just can't tell'" (229). In these pages, the theoretical utterances are reported in a briefer and more fragmentary manner than in the earlier seminar scene with Archie McCue, where fragments of his lecture are italicized, so we, like the students, cannot really make use of her utterances in our reading of *Emotionally Weird.*

There is, of course, a rich tradition of the satirical academic novel. Kingsley Amis's *Lucky Jim* and David Lodge's *Changing Places,* for instance, skewer university life from the faculty end of things (there is surely some of Amis's Professor Walsh in Atkinson's Professor Cousins, although the latter is less pompous and more endearing), while books such as Evelyn Waugh's *Decline and Fall* and Tom Sharpe's *Porterhouse Blues* tend to center on student life and, as happens in *Emotionally Weird,* contain an almost obligatory scene of alcohol and drug-fueled debauchery. In Atkinson's case, a party at Forres in Broughty Ferry (331–45) proves disorienting for Effie, who finds herself wandering a house that "must have been designed by Borges and constructed by Escher" (338), placing prostrate students in "the recovery position" (337, 339), and ending her evening waking in horror beside Dr. Dick, although she has no memory of how that happened. (Dr. Dick, an eighteenth-century literature specialist "who reveled in his hypochondria" [70], also aspires to be department head.) Also at the party, Effie saw Bob, her boyfriend, with "the *Finnegans Wake* girl . . . sprawled across his lap" (336). Effie had earlier spotted Bob with the same woman from the window of McCue's seminar room (49), but it is only later that we find out (in Agatha Christie fashion) what she saw: "On page 49 *I looked out of the third-floor window as if I'd just seen something interesting.* The thing I had seen was Bob, deep in conversation with one of Archie's postgraduate students, a young woman who was built like a pencil and whose doctoral thesis (*Losing the Plot*) was on *Finnegans Wake,* thus making her totally unsuitable for Bob" (152). Effie's last glimpse of him at the party "was in the massage room at Forres in the oily hands of the *Finnegans Wake* girl" (342). In rain and with "a wretched cold fog

. . . crawling in from the sea" and the melancholy sound of the foghorn booming—" ~ Can you have fog and rain at the same time? [Nora interrupts]. 'If I want.'" (341–42)—Effie leaves Dr. Dick. Shortly thereafter, ill and disoriented, Effie encounters a mysterious woman who claims to be the long, presumably drowned Effie (for whom Effie is named) and nearly drowns herself when, feverish and dizzy, she accidentally tumbles off a wharf, is saved by what she imagines is a mermaid, hospitalized, and then treated for the flu. Later she learns it was Effie who pulled her out of the water (370) and Ferdinand (Archie and Philippa's troubled son) who saved her (373). Finally, near the book's end, Effie discovers, through Nora and Chick's resolving tales, who her real mother and father were and are. Indeed, after her own near-death encounter (recalling a favored motif in romance but also Ruby's brush with the spirit world and Isobel Fairfax's hospital recovery), Effie is reborn to a new life.

How much we can trust these resolutions, though, is debatable and perhaps beside the point. In *Emotionally Weird,* all narrative is fiction and, as such, contingent on the whims of the teller. Effie's narrative is largely a plotless series of encounters (as Nora complains [186, 235]), but if something in the narrative is received poorly by the listener (often Nora) or even just inconvenient for the teller, the moment is reintroduced often with the identical language, now italicized, as was used the first time. In this respect, Atkinson is doing something similar to what she did in *Human Croquet* when Isobel relives Christmas Eve and Christmas morning numerous times. In *Emotionally Weird,* Effie finds herself in a snowstorm picked up by Ferdinand (281), but in a retelling it is Chick's car that stops (287). Olivia, a classmate and friend, in one telling dies of an overdose (365), but Nora objects: "No, no, no, no, *no,*' Nora says, very agitated,' you said this was a comic novel—you can't *kill* people" (365); in the revision Olivia is rescued by Effie and Kevin (366–67). Finally, when Jay Sewell falls over a banister to his death (while Effie, Terri, Andrea, and Chick are kidnapping Jay and Martha's dog), Effie revisits the scene, but in this case she finds a

> stray page of *The Expanding Prism of J* in which J plunges over the banisters and dies. . . . "Give me your lighter," I whispered urgently to Chick. . . . I grabbed it off him and set flame to the piece of paper in my hand . . . and turned [it] into a thin charcoal skin that floated up and hovered over the stairwell. . . . "Fucking hell," Chick said, looking down at the hall, "where's he gone?" For there was indeed no sign of a blood-boltered Jay, no screaming Martha, no sign of life or death. It was as if we had suffered a mass hallucination. "This is *so* freaky," Andrea said quietly. (329–30)

No explanation justifies this turn of events, although Effie says to Nora, who had used the term earlier (205), "Now *that's* magic realism" (330). Again, the story is in the teller's hands, and Atkinson breaks the illusion of fiction as mimesis. Indeed, we can't even say that Effie's revisions to her tale suggest alternatives for, as Chick remarks when he picks Effie up in the snowstorm, she has a large bruise on her forehead (288), which may have been caused by Ferdinand's car's door window which was slammed on Effie in the other narrative path (283).

Effie and Nora both acknowledge the fictional aspects of their stories and, like Scheherazade, both seek to hold the other's interest as they tell their tales to pass the time. Effie also acknowledges the comfort of Nora's voice (272). Nora's "strange and tragic" (379) tale is promised to be full of "murder and mayhem, plots and subplots, a madwoman in the attic, purloined diamonds, lost birthrights, heroic dogs, a soupçon of sex, a suspicion of philosophy" (26). And, indeed, it recalls many nineteenth-century novels of intrigue and family decline. Effie often observes about her family that "we are as jumbled as a box of biscuits" (251, 259, 380), and, indeed, they are.

Nora's promise of a "strange and tragic tale" full of sensation and murder is certainly borne out, though, despite the nod to *Jane Eyre,* there is no "madwoman in the attic" (391)—or, at least, no attic (but the older Effie is assumed to be mad). Nora's history is confusing partly because she identifies her relations in different ways. Initially, she speaks of Douglas as an older brother, of Euphemia (Effie) as an older sister, and of Lachlan as another of her older brothers. Douglas, though, is part of a slightly earlier generation of Stuart-Murrays: he is one of five children Donald fathered with his first wife, Evangeline. Two girls died in childhood and the three sons died in the First World War. Evangeline, distraught over the deaths of her children, hanged herself. Donald then married Marjorie, and four children result—Deirdre, who died as an infant, Lachlan, Euphemia, and, after fourteen years, Eleanora. Nora grows up believing Donald and Marjorie are her parents, but, in fact, Nora is the daughter of the incestuous coupling of her siblings Lachlan and Euphemia, who had Nora when she was fourteen. Nora grew up being treated as "defective—being in-bred" (379) because of her parentage. After the alcoholic Marjorie died prematurely, Donald, as an elderly man, remarried again; this time it was to Mabel, his housekeeper/nurse. She became mysteriously pregnant, though not by the infirm Donald. Deeply religious, Mabel found the pregnancy distressing. On the night Donald died, Mabel gave birth, and Nora, who was checking on Donald but finding him dead, heard Mabel's noises, ran to discover the baby, took it from Mabel, and then heard Effie returning. Only then did Nora see that Mabel, despairing of her sins, had ingested poison. Effie, always perceived as wild and out of control, arrives, assumes Nora is responsible for Donald's and Mabel's deaths, snatches the baby, with the intention of drowning what she fears is another heir to the family fortune, and during a chase jumps into a river where she struggles with the pursuing Nora. The baby is carried away in the current while Nora tries to drown Effie, who begs, "'Don't kill me, . . . I'm your mother'" (379). Nora assumes she has drowned Effie, finds the baby caught on a tree limb, and heads off to make a new life for herself because she fears the police will pursue her for murder. Nora and the baby lead a nomadic life until finally coming to the dilapidated Stuart-Murray vacation home. The final detail of note is that the father of Mabel's baby, who is our narrator Effie, is Chick, at the time a village policeman who had dropped in on Mabel one hot summer's day during jam season and, in a moment of mutual abandonment, fathered the child. Later, Chick participated in the investigation of the deaths in what became known as the Glenkittrie case. Euphemia, however, did not drown. She emerged naked from the river to be rescued by a man who sold women's shoes and who had come to the river to kill himself. The two of them recognized a "a fresh start. A re-birth" (387), and they moved to Rhodesia, where he started a successful business. His relatively recent death prompted Euphemia to return to Britain. This last part about Euphemia is narrated by Effie, who apparently heard the whole absurd tale from Euphemia before falling off the dock (379–80). Euphemia emerges in Nora's and Effie's narratives as the "madwoman" who had pursued Effie while uttering cryptic remarks about Nora being a murderess. Chick, as a private investigator, reveals that he was hired by Lachlan, who had died prior to this revelation, to find his daughter (Nora) and the baby. Lachlan had plucked Chick at random out of the yellow pages; his connection to the family and to Effie is pure coincidence, but "~ There's no such thing as coincidence, says my airy-fairy non-mother, draining her cup and glancing at her leftover tea-leaves" (388). In her 1999 afterword, Effie updates us on her friends and reports that she developed a relationship with Chick and her half-siblings (397), so, in fact, she does gain blood relations in the story, but learning her history means a secure sense of self is lost: "I would like my self to be given back to me. I would like a mother, father, brother, sister, aunt. . . . ~ Well, I can't give you *that,* Nora says, but I can tell you what happened" (385), and so Effie hears this marvelous tale which ends Nora's telling: "'No attic'" (391). Throughout the novel, Effie has moved from early on possessing a fairly secure sense of the self: "our self is the one thing we surely cannot lose . . . from the moment we are conceived it is the pattern in our blood and our bones are printed through with it like sticks of seaside rock," although Nora disagrees (24), to confusion. Later, Effie, like Alice in Wonderland, struggles, "I know who I *think* I am" (161), and finally she longs for her self to be given back to her. In the end, though, she has "gained [her] inheritance, which is to say, [her] blood. My mother was my mother, my father is my father" (391); but Nora, she acknowledges, will "always be my mother" (398).

It is a strange coming-of-age story and a convoluted family history that certainly challenges what we might mean by "family"; it is, dare we say, the stuff of fiction. Lachlan and Euphemia Stuart-Murray's intense incestuous relationship is clearly patterned on Heathcliff and Catherine's, while Donald's suspicious seeming death, Mabel's suicide, and Nora's escape with money, diamonds, and baby Effie conjures any number of sensation novels. Nora's story is calculated to hold Effie's and our interest: it doesn't have to be "true" or even plausible. The same can be said for Effie's humorous account of life at Dundee where the Brontës and George Eliot are openly discussed and, as student essays, traded among peers (360). Significantly, Effie struggles throughout her time in school to write a paper on *Middlemarch* for Professor Maggie Mackenzie, and sentences from that essay become part of the novel's discursive universe. (She is to discuss Henry James's judgement: "'*Middlemarch* is a treasure house of detail, but an indifferent whole'" [35].) Eliot and the Brontës mark poles in nineteenth-century fiction with the wild, gothic romance of the Brontës contrasted with the exemplary realism of *Middlemarch.*

One might be entitled to wonder if Effie's difficulties in discussing a realist novel are not somehow related to the amazing stories she and Nora tell. Eliot's and the Brontës' texts, however, are fiction too, and so are on a par with Nora's and Effie's narratives and with Kevin's fantasy novel, Andrea's loosely autobiographical fiction, Philippa's romance, Robin Lake's Beckettian play, and the rest. They're all just "words, words, words" (91), which bring back the many word games, beloved by Professor Cousins, such as "doublets," which he notes Lewis Carroll invented (95), and recall the book's opening epigraph from Carroll's *Through the Looking-Glass.*[17] Effie's narrating language is self-consciously playful in many places; for instance, "We all chose a different adverb to sup with. Philippa consumed her soup hungrily, Mrs MacBeth decided on messily, Mrs McCue on recklessly, whereas I myself opted for cautiously. Lucy Lake opted for not at all" (224); similar play takes place with adjectives (251), rhyming place names (331), and many other things. Readers, then, are put in the uncomfortable position of being encouraged to invest in narratives that repeatedly discourage that emotional investment by foregrounding language that reminds us we are reading fiction. We want the mystery of Effie's parentage, presented to us at the outset—"My mother is a virgin. (Trust me.)" (21)—solved, but its rapid resolution in Nora and Chick's concluding tales, although granting our desire and fulfilling the requirements of the comic form, is related by neither teller in a "realistic" manner. Instead, we get the artificiality of fairy-tale romance—especially in the discovery that Chick is Effie's father.

Emotionally Weird pushes Atkinson's ludic impulses to an extreme, but the foregrounding of language itself is common in all her novels. Before Effie's narrative even begins the opening two pages of "The Hand of Fate" question, as Isobel Fairfax did, everyday expressions and allude to a handful of authors (Agatha Christie and Raymond Chandler among them) and, anachronistically, to *Apocalypse Now,* while Madame Astarti, her amateur sleuth, has a name evoking pagan goddesses. Effie's story told to Nora is similar in its allusiveness and its linguistic play; clichés are examined and the discourse draws our attention to the mechanics of its telling and to its medium. Our response to *Emotionally Weird* may, then, be just that—essentially weird.

THREE

Short Fiction

Not the End of the World

That Kate Atkinson should have begun her career as a short story writer is not surprising; many novelists start this way, and Atkinson's doctoral dissertation was on postmodern American short stories. In her list of "Top Ten Books," originally printed in the *Guardian* but reprinted at the back of *Not the End of the World,* she singles out Coover's *Pricksongs and Descants* and Barthelme's *Collected Stories:* "Two of the most innovative of all American short story writers. Recklessly imaginative, they are both remarkable for the playfulness and sheer brio of their writing. Coover's ingenuity and Barthelme's absurdity made me look at writing in a different way. More than anyone else these are the writers who made me want to be a writer myself" (*Not the End,* Guide 9).[1] On the same list, she telling praised Vladimir Nabokov's "dizzyingly vertiginous prose" and Lewis Carroll's Alice books for their formative influence.[2] All of which goes to say that Atkinson's stories share in the adventurous playfulness of her precursors. Marvelous things happen (similar to Isobel becoming a tree), but the only constant is language.

Beginning in the early 1980s Atkinson found her moment with "In China," her first nonautobiographical piece and the first she submitted for publication. It won the *Woman's Own* short story prize in 1986.[3] She still counts this as her most treasured success: "It was the first time I'd had my writing validated, and the first thing I'd ever shown anyone" (Butki 2011). This success gave her the confidence to pursue her writing and, after her failure to gain a doctorate at the University of Dundee, proved a new tack was possible. Further success with short fiction followed; she was a runner-up in the Bridport Prize competition for short fiction in 1990 for a story that later became a chapter in *Behind the Scenes at the Museum;* and, most notably, "Karmic Mothers—Fact or Fiction?" won the Ian St. James Award in 1993 and was later adapted for a short film in

1997. *Behind the Scenes at the Museum* grew out of several stories that "had sat in a drawer for three years" (Parker 2002, 13). Other stories were published as well prior to 2002, several of which were dramatized for radio while others were worked into other pieces. "Leaves of Light," for example, from 1996, is a chapter in *Human Croquet.*

In 2002 she published *Not the End of the World,* which gathers a dozen pieces, some of which are interconnected, that develop Ovidian or otherwise classical transformations in the modern context. These are the experiments that freed her from the constraints of her first novels and "restor[ed] the joy that nestles at the heart of writing" ("Putting the Fun," 2003). Still, many of the stories have fantastical elements that suggest magic realism while also indulging in language games and postmodern narrative strategies. In the years since *Not the End of the World,* Atkinson has occasionally returned to the short story, offering stories for specific charities (Oxfam and Amnesty International) while also contributing to *Crimespotting,* a collection of crime fiction for an Edinburgh charity, and publishing an updating of *La Traviata* called "To Die For" to mark Glyndebourne Opera Festival's seventy-fifth anniversary. Most recently, three older Christmas-themed stories have been gathered as *Festive Spirits,* a slender volume with a share of the proceeds going to charity.

Unfortunately, several of Atkinson's short stories are unavailable. "In China," for example, though prize winning, has not been reprinted; *Woman's Own* remains based in the United Kingdom, but few libraries hold back issues.[4] Some early stories, such as "Karmic Mothers—Fact or Fiction" and "Inner Balance," are available in places that reprinted them, and others were worked into the early novels. Space does not permit comment on all of Atkinson's extant stories, and it is moot anyway to discuss tales that readers won't find. *Not the End of the World,* however, can be considered in greater detail.

Not the End of the World

As *Not the End of the World* took shape, Atkinson saw Charlene's and Trudi's stories ("Charlene and Trudi Go Shopping" and "Pleasureland") as "bookend[s] [for] the collection because essentially they are Scheherazade, telling the intervening stories to keep themselves alive" (*Not the End,* Guide 5) in the war-ravaged world they inhabit:

> "Tell me a story," [Trudi] said to Charlene.
>
> "I could tell you the story of the seven sisters who became the Pleiades."
>
> "I think we've had that one."
>
> "Marianne was thinking about lemons when she died?"
>
> "We've definitely had that one."
>
> . . .
>
> "Or how about Circe, who turned men into animals?"

> "No, I don't think I've heard that one."
>
> So Charlene told the story of the great witch Circe, and the story lasted all night long so that on the morning of the thousand and first day they were still awake when Helios left his magnificent eastern palace, with its columns of gold and bronze and its gables of ivory, . . . His sister, Eos, had already heralded his arrival, spreading her embroidered golden skirts across the skies.
>
> "Nothing dies," Charlene whispered into Trudi's ear. "All matter is transformed into other matter."
>
> "Or metempsychosis," Trudi said weakly, "the transmigration of the soul. Into an insect, a tadpole, a bean. A lion, a vine, a baby." (243–44)

In these final pages in the collection, we realize that many of the stories we have read are stories Charlene has told; the stories sustain, even create life in the sense that Charlene and Trudi are characters in stories. As is the case with Vladimir and Estragon in Samuel Beckett's *Waiting for Godot,* without words, there is nothing—the end of the world: "'Or we could just be quiet,' Charlene said. 'No,' Trudi said, beginning to panic, 'no, we mustn't do that'" (242).

In the above passage, the remark about Marianne thinking of lemons refers back to "Temporal Anomaly," in which Marianne is killed in a traffic accident, inhabits her family's house watching her husband and son, and then is returned to life some months later only to become another traffic fatality. Marianne's mother is not named in the story, although it becomes clear by the end that "Temporal Anomaly" is an adaptation in the present of the Demeter/Persephone myth—which is made explicit in Charlene's comments. Similarly, the above passage includes references to the Zane sisters, Jeri and Tyler, and to the seven sisters who became the Pleiades, which remind us of myth and of earlier stories: "Transparent Fiction" and "The Bodies Vest" include two of the sisters, Meredith and Nanci. The subject of "The Bodies Vest" is Vincent, who, while briefly married to Nanci Zane (she dies young during a dental procedure [188–89; 49]), thinks of the Zane sisters as being like the Pleiades (188). As is apparent, the stories in *Not the End of the World* often weave characters and events throughout the collection. A fatality on the M9, a major roadway in Scotland, is mentioned in a couple of places (103, 219), and we are inclined to see it as Marianne's accident, although its specific details are not mentioned elsewhere. Similarly, Romney Wright, whose son Arthur features in "Unseen Translation," is regarded as a tabloid celebrity in the world of many of the stories while the nanny, Missy, who takes care of Arthur, is a friend of Heidi's (from "The Cat Lover"), and Heidi is Trudi's twin sister (9, 241). Further connections abound, but there isn't narrative cohesion among the stories, so they do not form a sequence that might present a particular time and place. Instead, what binds them is the reworking of myth and classical tales of transformations (hence the reference to "metempsychosis" [244]). Ovid's opening lines provide the epigraph for *Not the End of the World*'s first story, "Charlene and Trudi Go Shopping":

> In nova fert animus mutatas dicere formas
> corpora, di, coeptis (nam vos mutastis et illas)
> adspirate meis primaque ab origine mundi
> ad mea perpetuum deducite tempora carmen (*Metamorphoses,* Book 1, lines 1–4[5]) (*Not the End of the World,* 2);

and for its last, "Pleasureland":

> Iamque opus exegi, quod nec Iovis ira nec ignis
> nec poterit ferrum nec edax abolere vetustas.
> cum volet, illa dies, quae nil nisi corporis huius
> ius habet, incert spatium mihi finiat aevi:
> parte tamen meliore mei super alta perennis
> astra ferar, nomenque erit indelibile nostrum.
> (*Metamorphoses,* Book XV, 871–6[6]) (*Not the End of the World,* 234).

So many of the stories work a bit like parts of *Human Croquet;* that is, contemporary characters find themselves intersecting strange worlds—just as in many of the Greek myths, gods interact with humans. (In *Human Croquet,* Isobel Fairfax is transformed into a tree and thus spared sexual violation, finds herself periodically visiting the past, and translates a passage from Ovid for school [146–47]). In stories such as "Tunnel of Fish" and "Unseen Translation," human figures encounter mythological beings: Eddie in "Tunnel of Fish" may have been fathered by Poseidon while Lester Goldman is married to a Lamian figure named Merle who, Meredith Zane discovers, owes her perpetual youthfulness to a reptilian cape she wears. Meredith snatches the cape at the end of the story and, unlike Atalanta, is undistracted by the golden apples at her feet and flees to avoid an ill-considered marriage. Again, connections among the stories are found: Eddie in "Tunnel of Fish" has a teacher, Mrs. McFarlane ("call me Pam" [32]), who we also encounter in "Wedding Favors" and earlier, through her children, in "Dissonance." Pamela is also the name of one of Bill Addison's daughters in "Sheer Big Waste of Love."

In narrative terms, these movements of characters among the stories offer another kind of transformation while in the stories themselves figures are revealed to be other than who or what they are: Eddie may be fathered by Poseidon, Marianne enacts Persephone's fate, Missy become Artemis, Bill Addison is a thundering Zeus. Not everyone, of course, corresponds so neatly, but many do. Atkinson's reworking of myth in contemporary settings is similar to the project of reworking fairy tales that she develops in *Human Croquet* and elsewhere. Her world then, however despoiled, corrupt, and strife-torn, is charged with the marvelous.

It is also worth noting that Atkinson reworks her own story material for different contexts. "Inner Balance" is, unlike much of her earliest work, available on the web.[7] If we look at it we can see how she used some of its narrative and description in her writing of "Tunnel of Fish"; indeed, "Inner Balance" offers another glimpse of a character in *Not the End of the World.* The earlier story, however, lacks the mythic, transformative plotting of those included in *Not the End of the World,* and so is not part of that collection. Instead, "Inner Balance" is structured around images of spiraling returns that on one level are evident in "the cast-iron staircase [that] turns like a stretched cochlea" and leads up to June and her son Alistair's apartment, in the curving interior of his shells, in the "spiralling down" of June's moods, and most significantly in the pink tunnel of the inner ear and particularly the cochlea that is crucial to hearing and to balance. Alistair's hearing is poor, and he "spends his time lost in his own private world of the half-deaf. June imagines it's like being on the ocean floor." The simile here, which occurs later as well, and Alistair's fascination with shells (he has a book about shells that he's read many times) again connect the story to "Tunnel of Fish," where June's son is named Eddie. In "Inner Balance" Mr. McFarlane, the specialist June takes Alistair to (and about whom she fantasizes) also has a large model of the inner ear in his consulting room that Alistair likes to take apart and reassemble. That the inner ear is crucial to our sense of balance gives the story's title its literal meaning, but possessing "inner balance" is also metaphorical as June is "working towards being a real person, balanced and healthy"—things that have proved challenging for her. To her dismay, she feels safest and most secure—balanced—in her childhood's bedroom, which is notable for the fact that "everything's pink": the curtains, carpet, bedding, even the brick work of the house, all resplendent in pink. The return to her parents' home is another curling back but on the level of the narrative, while the pinkness of the room suggests her own return to the seat of balance in a metaphorical inner ear. June feels at home here, but "it's horrible" because her feelings of security come at the price of knowing she has regressed.

In the collection, Charlene and Trudi use stories and language as compensation, as a means of survival, in a greatly reduced world. In the absence of significant food and drink, they feed themselves with words (much as Effie and Traci do in *Emotionally Weird* when they've nothing to eat for breakfast [33]): Charlene and Trudi imagine coffees (235–36) and other drinks (237) in the closing story. Similarly, objects are invested with symbolic importance to provide a rich imaginative content to meager surroundings. The various goods enumerated in "Charlene and Trudi Go Shopping" announce this project, but it is the

Sevres bowl, stolen from a museum in that story (15–16), that most clearly emphasizes my point: "All Trudi had in the house to eat was roasted buckwheat and celery. They served the buckwheat and celery in the Sevres bowl. 'Presentation is everything,' Charlene said" (16). When the substance is lacking, appearance becomes substantial. There is some absurdity in Charlene's and Trudi's efforts to maintain elements of cultural sophistication and fashion in a world where survival itself is threatened. Consequently, there is surely some black humor in Trudi's wave of jealousy when she sees a receptionist's "Heckler and Koch MP5 A3 9mm submachine gun under her desk" (9)—even the brand names of the weaponry can excite desire. Society may be crumbling into armed struggle, but the paradigm has not shifted. One could look at the situation as more evidence of how fragile civilization really is, but another way is to recognize that language and ritualized practice give meaning to a chaotic world—that, at least, may be the hope of Charlene and Trudi, who enumerate different kinds of honey, tea, dogs in an exercise that demonstrates a delight in both abundance and in language itself: words themselves become pleasing objects of attention. Trudi loves the word "dévoré" (3), and Charlene finds "Alhambra" "the most exotic word I can think of" (4). Language is reveled in not for its ability to represent a world but for its own sake, for its rhythms and sounds—as in the alliterative, "Bees the world over had been bamboozled out of their bounty" (4), or Trudi's enumeration of various fabrics, "Broadcloth and butter muslin, brocade, bocatelle, buckram, bunting, . . . ! And that's just the B's. Then, there's cambric and calico and cavalry twill—" (13). In this sense, the words become detached from the objects they name. The same can be said of the name brands associated with consumer goods (for example, "a Moschino dress and a Prada jacket and a Kenzo cardigan and a Gucci skirt . . . this Betty Jackson wrap" [12]). Charlene's and Trudi's attention to brands reminds us of the symbolic capital they possess that excites desire and, as with the receptionist's gun, jealousy. Again, it is not the thing so much as the word, the brand, that is valued. Language itself is viewed as thaumaturgical; hence the incantatory efforts to satisfy longing in the repetition of a word five times (as Trudi does with "kitty" [7]; a waitress, with "money" [9]; and even Heidi, in "The Cat Lover," with "baby" [165]).

Foregrounding language in the collection's opening story underscores the book's structure, which places Charlene and Trudi as the stories' tellers. They imagine Pleasureland, "where we would be gods" (18), and "Pleasureland" is the collection's final story. In between are ten stories anticipated in the Charlene's and Trudi's opening conversations; for example, Charlene imagines that she "would like a cat as big as a man" (8), which looks ahead to "The Cat Lover," where Trudi's twin sister, Heidi, meets such a creature. Similarly, Charlene's work on a bridal magazine means her articles, such as "Ten Things to Consider Before You Say 'I Do'" (5), are read by others such as Addison Fox's fiancée,

Claire, in "Sheer Big Waste of Love" (92). Charlene also attends wedding trade shows, such as the one where Pam and Maggie exhibit their *bomboniere* in "Wedding Favors." As Atkinson explained, "The first few of these stories were commissioned; I . . . found they were becoming intertwined. It was very important to me that each story stood alone, but as I went on I found that thin, spider web-like connections began to form" ("Putting the Fun").

Writing these stories allowed Atkinson "a watershed between what is essentially the trilogy of my first three books and whatever is to come after" ("Putting the Fun"). From our vantage point, we know that what came after was the Brodie novels. Nonetheless, the fantastical elements in the stories, their overt allusiveness (especially to myth), and the web of connections they develop are all qualities that her novels share. In the stories, we see the intersection of the mythic with the mundane, the classical with the contemporary. "Transparent Fiction" ends with the fleeing Meredith Zane "sidestepping the golden apples lying in her path" (60). "Unseen Translation" concludes with Arthur's vision: Missy's "sensible leather boots had turned into silver sandals. . . . For a few dizzying seconds Arthur saw the quiver of silver arrows on Missy's back, gleaming in the moonshine" (132). Missy, we understand, has become Artemis. Even passages and phrases of description show classical antecedents, "Heidi awoke when Eos's rosy raiments cover the sky" ("The Cat Lover" 173), while in "Unseen Translation," again, Arthur and Missy sleep "long after the dawn had scattered her yellow robes across the skies" (127), and the book's concluding passage quoted earlier demonstrates the same point. "Sheer Big Waste of Love" links Bill Addison to Zeus ("he came in a fucking shower of gold" [91]); when the young Addison and his mother enter the yard at Bill Addison's house, the boy has "a vision of an unearthly kingdom, peopled by heavenly creatures" (99). Bill Addison's violent response to the interruption of Addison and his mother is accompanied by a sudden thundershower (102). These and other references illuminate the mundane world by drawing attention to its magical elements. Even Pam's daughter Rebecca in "Dissonance" can bring a man back to life—with first aid training and CPR (82–83). Atkinson's range of allusions in the stories, as the epigraphs preceding them demonstrate, extends beyond classical myth and canonical literature to popular culture at large—*Buffy, the Vampire Slayer, Star Trek: Voyager,* Mary Poppins, Harry Potter, and others, to say nothing of the many brand-named consumer goods that Charlene and Trudi enumerate—and confirm the "presentness" of the stories. Their world is the milieu of the early years of this century; myth sparks imagination: Eddie in "Tunnel of Fish," Arthur in "Unseen Translation," Meredith Zane in "Transparent Fiction" are all inspired by their encounters with classical deities.

Ultimately, despite their interconnectedness, the stories do stand on their own. And while their endings may not always be happy ones, they offer closure if sometimes of an indeterminate sort. In "Dissonance," Rebecca, who aspires to a career in medicine, is shaken by the responsibility of preserving life (83), while her brother Simon, whose hostility toward his mother, Pam, has been extreme (63), finds her presence comforting when he is hospitalized after a serious accident (81–82). Such reversals render the title meaningful on a level beyond the musical reference to the concert Rebecca attends. In "Wedding Favors" Pam feels sad and uncertain as the story ends, while Addison in "Sheer Big Waste of Love" (a title that mirrors a student essay's conclusion about *Romeo and Juliet* that Pam marks in "Dissonance" [68]) expresses compassion for the half-siblings, especially Susan, who all suffered the tyranny of their father (Susan even suggests her sister Pamela was abused by him [108]) and who are unaware of his relationship to them. At the very end of that melancholy piece, Susan watches Addison leave and we wonder, although there is no evidence, whether she remembered him as the young boy she felt compassion for who had come with his mother to confront his father. Of course, the stories do end, and there is a kind of narrative satisfaction that each provides. As Atkinson said of the collection, "With novels, I'm very aware that I'm always looking for redemption for the characters. I want them to have endings, and preferably satisfactory ones where good and evil are rewarded and punished in some way. When I write stories I feel liberated from this compulsion—I can leave things unresolved, allow the edges to be blurred and abandon characters to unhappiness" ("Putting the Fun"). Are the endings of her stories always plausible? No. Meredith Zane, donning a cloak that will extend her life? Heidi, pregnant with kittens? Marianne's on again off again life cycle? These are fantastical endings. Others, with Pam, Addison, Simon, and Rebecca, are perhaps more realistic. More importantly, though, is the imaginative verve Atkinson inherited from authors she studied, especially Coover, whose *Pricksongs and Descants* "changed [her] life" and led her "to the writers who had been there all the time—Borges, Barth, Vonnegut, and onward to the wonderful world of Barthelme" (Introduction to *Pricksongs* 5). "Pleasureland" is dedicated to Barthelme, and the stories in *Not the End of the World* amply demonstrate how she absorbed their lessons.

FOUR

Detective Fiction

The Jackson Brodie Novels

It is not by chance that Effie in *Emotionally Weird* should assert to her creative writing instructor, Martha Sewell, that detective fiction is "a postmodernist kind of thing these days" (56), for since the advent of structuralism in literary study, detective fiction has become a genre highly amenable to theoretical analysis. Tzvetan Todorov explicitly used detective fiction to illustrate narrative principles, and many other structuralist and poststructuralist theorists from Lacan to John Irwin to Peter Brooks have found the genre's explicit self-consciousness and metaphoric, even literal, representation of reading and interpretation useful.[1] The detective story "thematizes narrativity itself as a problem, a procedure, and an achievement" (Hühn 1987, 451); more explicitly, it is "the narrative of narratives, its classical structure a laying-bare of the structure of all narrative" (Brooks 1984, 25). The investigator, like the reader, examines/reads clues to reconstruct the meaning of a narrative that is hidden; at the same time, this reconstruction uncovers another story. It is a tale as old as Oedipus's quest.

Many modernist and postmodernist writers such as Jorge Luis Borges, Thomas Pynchon, and Paul Auster have exploited the genre, and their efforts, coupled with poststructuralist arguments that undermine hierarchical binaries, have worked to disarm some of the critical prejudice against genre fiction that Effie, a character situated in the early 1970s, worried about. It is often the case now that literary authors will work with the conventions of genre fiction, if not write a piece of genre fiction, without employing pseudonyms (as C. Day-Lewis, J. I. M. Stewart, and Carolyn Heilbrun did, for example) or dismissive epithets (such as Graham Greene's "an entertainment"). Of course, pseudonyms are still employed (Booker winner John Banville writes crime fiction under the name of Benjamin Black), but increasingly writers are less worried about working in areas traditionally thought of as "genre fiction." It is not necessarily surprising that Kate Atkinson, who played with explicitly self-conscious narration in her first novels and stories should turn to detective fiction. Indeed, the move was signaled in *Emotionally Weird* in the character of Chick, the private investigator, and in Effie's own creative work.

Following the publication of *Not the End of the World,* Atkinson's next four novels all featured an investigator, Jackson Brodie, who, with help, discovers the solutions to multiple mysteries (but not all). The first of these books, *Case Histories,* appeared in 2004; it was followed by *One Good Turn* (2006), *When Will There Be Good News?* (2008), and *Started Early, Took My Dog* (2010). A fifth volume in the series, *Big Sky,* appeared in 2019. While each book can be read on its own, as a series the action of each picks up a couple of years (or almost ten, in the case of the last) after the previous volume's story. Hence, besides Jackson, some characters do recur, such as Julia, who first appears in *Case Histories* and becomes romantically involved with Jackson at the end of that novel, and Marlee, Jackson's daughter. As do Atkinson's other books, the Brodie stories deal with gender, genre, and the problem of virtuous action in a morally ambiguous world. These books often include moments we associate with the genre (Jackson is knocked unconscious, a body disappears, the police are suspicious of him, etc.), but Atkinson builds her novels around characters and their relationships: "'It's not about crime, you have to understand,' Julia said. 'It's about them as *people.*' 'They're not real,' Jackson pointed out.' 'I know that. Art *renders* reality'" (*Started Early,* 179). Because Atkinson is interested in developing the characters, many of her figures are given a depth that hints at mysteries in their own pasts. If we think of Theo Wray or Amelia Land in *Case Histories,* Matilda "Tilly" Squires in *Started Early, Took My Dog,* to say nothing of Jackson's own development as the series goes on, we realize how much space in the narratives is devoted to characters' thoughts, concerns, and behaviors that are unrelated to the main story lines: Caroline's flirtation with the vicar in *Case Histories;* Louise's relationship with her son, Archie, and her attachment to her cat, Jelly Bean; and the background information about Reggie's past life or even about Joanna Hunter's father, Howard Mason—all hint at stories untold.

In interviews, when she was asked about her turn to writing a male protagonist, Atkinson remarked, "It's been said that the men in my books have been absent, or weak, or creepy. Jackson is 'the last good man standing'" (Brown 2004). Elsewhere, she noted, Jackson is "secretly a woman. He's my authorial voice. I just use him as me" (Fox 2011). (However, about *One Good Turn,* she claimed, "Gloria is me. . . . She's the closest to me of all characters I've ever written" [Scribner 2006].) Saying Jackson is "secretly a woman" is a bit flip, but the novels do question notions of masculinity in the character and in the genre. Jackson often wonders if he is behaving as a woman would (*One Good Turn,* 127), and Julia suggests, "The older you get, the more like a woman you become" (*Started Early,* 50). Jackson feels the money he surprisingly inherited from a former client in *Case Histories* "unmanned" him because "Real men had to earn a hard crust" (*One Good Turn,* 37). But even in *Case Histories,* Jackson's friend Howell teases Jackson, "What happened, have you turned into a woman?" (267), and a page later Jackson responds jokingly, "I'm a policeman, I've turned into a woman, I'm pussy whipped, and I carry and organ-donor card. It's called middle age" (268). This exchange, though, picks up on similar statements made in a few places in *Case Histories.* Although Atkinson plays with hard-boiled clichés-"Trouble is my friend" (*One Good Turn,* 273) and, "People who asked for his help always lead him down paths he didn't want to tread. Paths that lead to the town called Trouble" (*Good News* 260)-Jackson is more soft-boiled.[2] Like Chandler's Philip Marlowe, Jackson is a romantic idealist: "despite everything he'd seen and done, inside Jackson there remained a belief-a small, battered and bruised belief-that his job was to help people be good rather than punishing them for being bad" (*Case Histories* 53). *Case Histories* foregrounded mysteries, which are a part of all Atkinson's writing: "I was aware when I wrote *Case Histories* that it would be perceived as crime fiction. But I didn't feel I was writing a crime novel. It was just my novel with crime in it" (Scribner 2006). Certainly, from the point of view of Atkinson's overall technique, the Brodie novels continue her practice of developing intertwining narratives within a single novel. *Case Histories,* for instance, presents three—or four, if we recall Jackson's sister—different crimes occurring in different periods (1970, 1971, 1979, and 1994) while the present is assumed to be roughly 2004 (chapter headings alert us to these shifts backward and forward in time through the dates and relevant characters).[3] And the Brodie books continue to display the author's characteristic wit and, in a slightly reduced fashion, her recognition of all writing taking place within a literary realm. That is, allusions to other texts underscore character and events while self-consciously reminding us the books are fiction.

As a series, the novels after *Case Histories* can and do refer to details in their predecessors, and they can be said to occur in "real" time; hence, events in *One Good Turn* (2006) take place roughly two years after those of *Case Histories.* Hence, we see the characters' relationships develop through time—a circumstance that has the unhappy consequence of leaving readers at the end of *Started Early, Took My Dog* (2010) wondering about Jackson's future, particularly how it might include Louise Monroe, a police inspector introduced in *One Good Turn,* who is teasingly presented as a potential love interest.[4] *Big Sky* picks up Jackson and several characters from earlier Brodie books (Reggie, Tatiana, Julia, for instance) about ten years later, but Louise Monroe is absent except in memory and a brief moment at the end. *Big Sky,* published too late to take a full accounting of here, fits uneasily with the earlier books in the series because of its temporal distance, so the links to prior events can occasionally appear forced.

Jackson Brodie, we find out in *Case Histories,* entered the Prince of Wales's Own Regiment of Yorkshire as a teenager, later served in the military police, joined Cambridge police after leaving the military, and then started a career as a private investigator. Near the beginning of *One Good Turn* we learn he has sold his investigator business and spends much of his time in France (33). He is divorced from Josie, has a daughter, Marlee (aged ten in *One Good Turn,* eight in *Case Histories,* on the verge of marriage in *Big Sky*). In *One Good Turn* he has been in a relationship with Julia Land for two years, although it appears to be on shaky ground and is over by the novel's end, when Julia reveals she is pregnant but not with Jackson's child. Jackson's first appearance in *When Will There Be Good News* (2008) has him watching a group of children and surreptitiously gathering hair fibers from a small boy named Nathan, who turns out, indeed, to be Jackson's son. In *Started Early, Took My Dog,* Jackson does spend time with Nathan and Julia, but there isn't any hope of a family reunion. Otherwise, Jackson has no family, we learned in *Case Histories,* because his mother died when he was twelve, his father more recently, and, most significantly for him, his older sister, Niamh, was murdered. An older brother, Francis, guilt stricken for not having picked his sister up after work in bad weather on the night she disappeared (259), hanged himself six months after the murder (263). Jackson is also haunted by guilt (which is jokingly attributed to his Catholicism [*One Good Turn,* 91–92; 159]) and half-seriously wonders if he is cursed: "'Believe me [Reggie says], bad things happen to me all the time.' 'Me too,' Jackson said" (*Good News* 297). In all five novels, he is especially worried about the dangers that men pose to women and girls, and "he [will] go on looking for all the lost girls, the Olivias, the Joannas, the Lauras. And his sister, Niamh, the first lost girl" (*Started Early* 47). His thoughts often tend this way, and it is clear that Niamh's unsolved murder is the crime that stands behind every crime Jackson investigates: "'Really you're looking for your sister,' Julia said. 'Your own dear grail. You're never going to find her, Jackson. She's gone'" (*Started Early* 47). Every case, then, is only imperfectly solved ("half the equation is better than none" [47]). There is no doubt that professional and personal experiences have exacerbated his concerns, so he worries particularly about Marlee (*Case Histories,* 115, 117), which allows Atkinson to have him reflect on the sexualization of children and its links to patriarchal fantasies of dominance (117).

Other characters who have experience in the police have similar worries. In *Started Early, Took My Dog* Tracy is deeply aware of the vulnerability of children, especially girls: "Nothing innocent. Anywhere" (163, 166, elsewhere). In taking on the care of Courtney, an abused child, she would partially "make up for all the other lost kids" (84). And when Louise Monroe thinks about how Jackson wants to find all the missing girls ("holy girls" in *Case Histories*), she contrastingly imagines that she doesn't "want them to get lost in the first place. There were a lot of ways of getting lost, not all of them involved being missing. Not all of them involved hiding, sometimes women got lost right there in plain sight" (*Good News* 122). (Louise is thinking about Alison Needler "disappearing inside her own marriage," but a character such as Lily-Rose from *Case Histories* is another woman who disappears in plain sight: Lily-Rose, we discover, is the Tanya that Jackson is asked to search for at one point.) All these women, Louise considers, deserve medals (116–17). As a detective, Jackson easily identifies with victims and with their family members. Significantly, in *When Will There Be Good News,* his catalog of family loss is matched by Joanna Hunter's, although the circumstances differ, and Julia Land's family history has parallels with Jackson's as well—Jackson and Julia are both "freakishly bereaved" (*Good Turn,* 60). Unavoidably, investigating crimes that involve the search for young girls and women takes Jackson into his past and reenacts, in a sense, an original trauma. When Louise tells him in *One Good Turn,* "You see dead girls everywhere," his reply is chillingly ironical: "No, I see the same dead girl everywhere" (273). Even as he reads an Alex Blake novel prior to meeting Martin Canning at a book festival (in what may be a nod to C. Day-Lewis, Alex Blake is Canning's pseudonym), his thoughts drift to Niamh's funeral, which he could not bring himself to attend (320): "What he *had* felt for most of his life was that he was living on in the aftermath of a disaster, in the endless postscript of time that was his life following the murder of his sister and the suicide of his brother. . . . Those terrible feelings . . . formed the hard, black nugget of coal at the heart of his soul" (*Good News,* 283). As with many literary detectives, and the same is true of Ruby Lennox and Isobel Fairfax, the drive to solve his cases is rooted in trauma. Significantly, the metaphor here is a "nugget of coal": Jackson's father worked in a coal mine and refused to allow Jackson to follow him into the pit, so Jackson joined the army.

In imagining Jackson Brodie, Atkinson was able to draw on any number of precursors, but the Edinburgh setting in two Brodie books—perhaps reflecting Atkinson's own move to the city—unavoidably calls to mind Ian Rankin's John Rebus. Superficially, Rebus and Brodie have much in common: they are both ex-military, divorced with a daughter, and fond of particular kinds of music that is often remarked on (although Jackson prefers country music), and they are both individualists who nonetheless work or worked within the structure of the police. Rankin is a leading figure in what has come to be known as "tartan noir," and Atkinson clearly acknowledges his example in the Brodie books when Reggie Chase, in *When Will There Be Good News?,* watches *Rebus* on television. Rankin himself commented on *One Good Turn* in the *Guardian:* it "is *the most fun I've had with a novel this year.* It's a convoluted murder mystery set in Edinburgh during the height of the festival season, and features a wimpish crime writer who better not be based on me" (Hooker 2006; my italics note the part that appears as a promotional blurb on the paperback of *One Good Turn*). Rankin repaid Atkinson's allusion to Rebus in his *Even Dogs in the Wild* (2015) where Siobhan Clarke, Rebus's long time partner and friend, reads a novel while the police await the possible appearance of a suspected killer: Rebus asks, "'What's the book?' 'He said, changing the subject. It's Kate Atkinson.' 'Any good?' 'Someone keeps coming back from the dead.' 'Not a bad fit for this evening, then'" (310). The book is clearly *Life After Life.* (Interestingly, in *Transcription,* Juliet Armstrong receives threatening anonymous notes—"You will pay for what you did" [186 and elsewhere]; in *Even Dogs in the Wild* figures targeted for murder also receive threatening anonymous notes—"I'm going to kill you for what you did" [75 and elsewhere])

"Fun" might be an odd descriptor for a story that involves so much violence, but Atkinson does give *One Good Turn* a subtitle, "A Jolly Murder Mystery," and a kind of comical absurdity often shades the violence. Martin Canning, the "wimpish crime writer," often hears the remembered voice of his abusive father in his thoughts (115; 286), but he also daydreams about being in an old-fashioned marriage (254 and elsewhere), and even his fictional detective, Nina Riley, intrudes into his thinking in moments of peril with her archaic phrasing (258). These moments exemplify aspects of the book's absurdities, while a self-consciousness about the genre highlights others. There is, of course, the contrast between Martin Canning's stories featuring Nina Riley and her sidekick, Bertie (who invert the Peter Whimsey / Harriet Vane dyad of Dorothy Sayers's series), and the "reality" of Canning's connection to Richard Moat's murder by Terence Smith in Canning's apartment. (Smith thought Moat was Canning, and, because Moat was wearing Canning's wristwatch, the police thought the same, which causes a good deal of ironic comment from the police [218], newspapers [236–38], and others about a mystery writer being involved in a real murder.) But there are also many references to other detective novels: a pathologist is named Ackroyd (180); "A murder is announced" (236; the title of a 1950 Agatha Christie novel); "Was that really a suitable job for a woman?" Jackson asks Louise Monroe (he's referring to a "living statue of Marie Antoinette," but the phrasing recalls P. D. James's first Cordelia Gray novel, *An Unsuitable Job for a Woman* [248]). Similar things can often be found in crime fiction, and likewise in the other Brodie novels. For instance, in *When Will There Be Good News?,* one of Louise's colleagues remarks, "It's like something out of Agatha Christie" (278), and the same character, Sandy Mathieson, earlier says, "Surely that only happens in TV crime shows, not real life" (207). Late in *One Good Turn,* Jackson finds that "Moviespeak . . . seemed to make Martin happy" (323, also 311), and later still, Jackson imagines he's part of "some new kind of reality television show" (338) when a number of characters are gathered in Gloria Hatter's living room as Smith, "the Honda Man," bursts in with a baseball bat.

At this point, the appearance of another figure, Martin Canning, is confusing for Smith,

> apparently from the effort of trying to work out why all the people he wanted to kill were in the same room together. . . . He [Jackson] wondered vaguely what the other people in the room were doing while he was waiting to have his skull broken open. Surely Tatiana could do something useful with her knife? And failing that she could rip open Terence Smith's throat with her teeth. She was doing neither, he could hear her on the phone, speaking in Russian, very fast. He wondered what she was saying. Send lawyers, guns, and money? (339)

On multiple levels the passage distances readers from the seriousness of the confrontation. Smith, elsewhere described as "The Incredible Hulk on steroids," "the Minotaur" (129), and the "golem" (336), is clearly barbarous, while Tatiana, whose cold-hearted skills suggest, for one reviewer, a Bond villain (although she's also described as being "like a comedy Russian" [Craig 2006, 335]), is always in control of her situation. Jackson sees her as a wolf who would have made an exceptional spy in a previous regime or possibly an assassin, "Maybe she still was" (323). The gathering of characters points to the narrative's self-conscious construction and its heavy plotting. The many disparate narrative threads are again coming together: "Everything was connected. Everything in the world" (337). In fact, they are reconnecting; for, as the paragraph reminds us, almost all of the book's principle characters were present at the opening scene when Smith, who was driving a blue Honda, used his bat on Paul Bradley, which is that character's assumed name. This opening centers a web of stories that intersect as we come to discover how many of the key characters saw all or part of the assault.[5]

The metaphor the text supplies for this narrative structure is the *matryoshka*, the Russian dolls that nest inside each other: "Secrets within secrets. Dolls within dolls" (261). Jackson, who is leaving one of Julia's rehearsals; Gloria and Pam, who are in a ticket line; Martin Canning, also in line; Louise's son Archie and his friend Hamish, running from a shop—all see some part of Smith's assault on "Paul Bradley," and each then has a distinct narrative arc that is developed in occasionally intersecting chapters. Gloria's friend Pam, for instance, attends Martin's public reading and book signing; Louise shares her worries about Archie with Jackson (271); Martin later calls Jackson (286), who had given the distressed man his mobile number after Martin had thrown his briefcase at "the Honda man" who was about to bludgeon Bradley (38). Smaller details weave among the different stories too; for instance, police constable Claire Deponio, with her partner, visits Gloria to tell her of her husband's heart attack (67), but Deponio is also assigned to look after Manning after Richard Moat's death (231), and she was one of those who helped Bradley after the assault (231). Later, she is one of the team of officers who arrives at Gloria's residence after Martin shoots Smith (345): all the dolls—all the story arcs—back together temporarily until the narrative scatters them into separate resolutions that in some cases lead to more questions: what of Julia's baby? Gloria's ties to Tatiana and also to Paul Bradley?

The idea that everything is connected is commonly implied in mystery stories and is a staple in classical detective stories of the Poe, Doyle, Christie variety, where metaphors of a puzzle or a chain are invoked to explain the detective's reasoning. (These are the sort of stories Canning is said to write.) Implicitly, this form of the genre suggests a universe whose workings are discernible to the reasoning observer: as Sherlock Holmes argues, "all life is a great chain. . . . By a man's finger nails, by his coat-sleeve, by his boot, by his trouser knees, . . .—by each of these things a man's calling is plainly revealed" (Doyle 1930, 23). Atkinson's Brodie novels are less assured, but Jackson, like Perry in *Transcription* (129), does not trust coincidence and even invokes the metaphor of the "chain of evidence" when pondering the "karmic concatenation" that connects him to Julia (*One Good Turn,* 291; he uses the same metaphor in *When Will There Be Good News?* 89). "A coincidence," Jackson tells Louise in a recurring line in the Brodie novels, "is just an explanation waiting to happen" (246; *Good News,* 157). (In developing a kind of doppelganger for Jackson in *Started Early, Took My Dog,* Atkinson has Brian Jackson, another private investigator, tell Tracy, "I always say that a coincidence is just an explanation waiting to happen" [293].) The turn from coincidence to connection is explicit in Jackson's investigations. Nonetheless, in Atkinson's novels, contingency and coincidence often supplement Jackson's reasoning. As one of its epigraphs suggests, *Started Early, Took My Dog* turns heavily on chance, a fact we are reminded of by a repeated line from the epigraph, "For want of a nail" (56, 57, 63, etc.).

There is, though, something paradoxical about the notion of chance being foregrounded in a plotted novel, where presumably from the writer's point of view chance does not really exist. Indeed, narrative fundamentally works to reduce chance and contingency to pattern and connection. Atkinson acknowledges this problem in Jackson's conviction that coincidence will resolve into connection but she also more self-consciously addresses the issue early in *Started Early, Took My Dog,* when Jackson unaccountably ends up rescuing a dog from an abusive owner: "He had not expected to walk away a dog owner. The interrupted journey, the unexpected gift, the unforeseen encounter. Life had its plots" (63). Whether life has its plots or whether plots are imposed upon life is precisely the question, and maybe the two cannot really be separated. Jackson ends up with a dog by chance, but within the structure of the novel his acquisition of the dog parallels Tracy's acquisition of Courtney, who is also taken from an abusive caretaker. Both Jackson and Tracy, of course, are ex-police—another coincidence that resolves into a connection. What are presented as impulsive, unmotivated actions on one level are on another the product of careful plotting.

Still, the novels often leave us with enigmatic and puzzling details—such as the surprising revelation that Gloria hired Paul Bradley to kill her husband in *One Good Turn;* Joanna Hunter's equally surprising acquisition of a gun from Reggie's brother Billy in *When Will There Be Good News?;* and the mysterious phone calls Tracy Waterhouse receives in *Started Early, Took My Dog.* In *Case Histories* we never learn if Theo Wray reads the name of his daughter's murderer that Jackson has written on a postcard for him. Caroline disappears (with the vicar?), and we never learn why her negligent sister, Shirley, is looking for Tanya. Jackson is saved on at least two occasions in *One Good Turn* by surprisingly random events: one is Canning's timely appearance with a gun and his killing of Smith (readers are completely surprised that Canning even has the gun); another involves the death of Smith's dog as it charges a battered Brodie (apparently, it collapses because of a heart attack or stroke). These sorts of details tell readers that things are not so serious. Typically, too, the narrative incorporates a fair amount of humor in the characters' banter that contribute to the book's jolly fun.

Also appealing is the range of allusions and references we find in the text. Some are attributed to the fact that a few characters have studied English literature (and such characters can be found in virtually all of Atkinson's books); hence, Gloria once gave her husband, Graham, "a beautifully illustrated Folio society copy of the collected poems [of Percy Bysshe Shelley] for his sixtieth birthday, on the basis that you should give a present you would like to receive yourself" (277). Significantly, Graham misreads "Ozymandias" as triumphant and uses the title for his business accounts' computer password. Gloria's daughter Emily has a master's degree in literature from Goldsmiths, "and it made her into the kind of person who used critique as a verb" (210), and Louise, "graduated from St Andrews with a first in English" and was encouraged "to do an M Phil but what was the point, really?" (147).[6] Atkinson's "jolly murder mystery" continues practices that were more obviously employed in her first three books. We find varied modes of discourse, references to numerous other texts, self-reflexive discussion, and even a fantastical incident when Nina Riley, his literary creation, takes leave of Canning.

Like Effie in *Emotionally Weird,* Canning writes detective stories with titles such as *The Monkey-Puzzle Tree* and *Death on the Black Isle,* and, as in *Emotionally Weird,* text from the detective stories dot *One Good Turn* in italicized font, particularly in moments of contrast such as when Canning returns to his apartment after Moat's murder (196). Canning tends to think of this unabashedly nostalgic work as hack writing, and he aspires to a literary masterpiece, which means *One Good Turn* raises questions about the nature of genre fiction as opposed to other kinds of work. The point is implicit in *Emotionally Weird* and foregrounded again in *Started Early, Took My Dog.*

A mystery writer's presence in a mystery novel is hardly unusual—indeed, Marilyn Nettles in *Started Early, Took My Dog* writes crime novels under the pseudonym Stephanie Dawson. In *One Good Turn* Atkinson is able to use this feature of the genre to enhance her discursive play. Canning's involvement in a "real" murder boosts attendance at a public reading. (Gloria's friend Pam is there and purchases two signed copies of the most recent Alex Blake book for herself and Gloria [335–36].) As the book goes on, we learn Canning is a dreamy, timid figure who was bullied growing up by an abusive ex-military father. He is also plagued by guilt stemming from an encounter with a Russian prostitute named Irina while on vacation in St. Petersburg that resulted in her accidental death. Details emerge piecemeal, but Canning suffers hallucinating delusions prior to and after killing Smith. He hears Irina, presumably because she alone refers to him as "Marty," say, "'Shoot him, Marty.' So he did" (352). Later, in a brief chapter 53 that recalls some of the more fantastical elements found in *Human Croquet,* Nina Riley decides she must kill herself for Martin's sake. Typographically, the italicized text now shows medical people discussing Martin's gibbering state; the Riley portion is in the novel's usual font: the fictional character has entered the discourse as a real character (albeit in Martin's imagination, which is now his only reality). The recollection of *Human Croquet* here is not an isolated moment in *One Good Turn.* Elsewhere, Gloria's eye catches a flicker in her garden. Peering through binoculars, she sees "the glossy, green leaves . . . revealing a face, Ovidian amongst the greenery. . . . At any rate she was sure now that it wasn't a bear or a horse. Nor was it a woman metamorphosed into a tree" (204). The allusion is doubly pointed to not only Ovid's *Metamorphoses* but to the earlier novel as well.[7]

Atkinson's playfulness extends into passages of description—"A miasma of Usher-like doom seemed suddenly to rise up and fold itself around the house like a wet shroud. Death had stalked its rooms. He had a terrible headache. Death had found him" (198); of dialogue, "'I see dead people,' Jessica intoned" (217) or "'An inspector calls,' Gloria said" (336); in naming, Ackroyd is the pathologist (180); and in general lines of discourse, "Hey, Knox, leave that kid alone" (101).[8] These and other references provide the alert reader with another level of enjoyment while underscoring the cool distance Atkinson's narrators typically keep from events: "'*Graham* forgot his *phone*?' 'I know, it's hard to believe, but there you go. Astonishing things happen all the time.' (It was true, they did.)" (118–19). One might locate the parenthetical comment in Gloria's consciousness (we certainly are apprised of much of her thinking about animals, her brother's death, her general situation, but not about everything, as the ending makes clear), but its appearance in the discourse recalls instances of similar interruptions in Atkinson's work, and so we take it as typical of her narrative technique which foregrounds the storytelling. Atkinson's novels, as she later says, "are not only fiction but they are about fiction too" ("Author's Note" to *God in Ruins,* 387), and the Brodie novels are no exception. A telling moment near the end of *Started Early, Took My Dog* presents a puzzle similar to the one posed by the parenthetical comment after Gloria's excuse for Graham's absence. Jackson is saying goodbye to Julia and Nathan at Manchester airport, and Jackson is overwhelmed with love for his son: "It just went to show, you never knew what you were going to feel until you felt it. It was terrifying, although Julia would have said 'wonderful,' being the full half of the glass. 'Stop putting words in my mouth,' Julia said" (339). Julia's remark does not follow from the brief conversation the two have so the question arises: who is she addressing? Jackson's thought? or perhaps the narrator itself who, of course, does put words in all the characters' mouths?

In *When Will There Be Good News?,* Reggie (Regina) Chase is deliberately presented in chapter titles and in the discourse as the plucky orphan investigator of girls' adventure stories; as she rushes toward a train wreck, our narrator ends the chapter, "What larks, Reggie!" (130). Later we read, "Who was she? She was the Famous Reggie, she was Regina Chase, Girl Detective, she was Virgo Regina, the storm-tossed queen of the plucky abandoned orphans" (229). (We could almost be in the world of the Augustus books that we hear about in *Life After Life* and, especially, *A God in Ruins.*) And Dickensian chapter titles cue us to Reggie's character as well: "The Life and Adventures of Reggie Chase, Containing a Faithful Account of the Fortunes, Misfortunes, Uprisings, Downfallings, and Complete Career of the Chase Family" (30); other chapter titles are "The Famous Reggie" (162) and "Reggie Chase, Girl Detective" (174). Still others are more allusive: "She Would Get the Flowers Herself" (64), "A Clean, Well-lighted Place" (316), "Great Expectations" (324), "A Good Man is Hard to Find"(234), and "The Discreet Charm of the Bourgeoisie" (113) (the last reference to Luis Buñuel's film, explained forty pages later [153]). Again, allusions and plot details connect this book to others, often in a similar genre. One could multiply examples, but the point is clearly made: we read the novels aware of their status as stories.

For Atkinson, the detective genre satisfies a desire for narrative resolution, but it also contains other concerns. As Jonathan Dee (2018) recently notes in a discussion of *Transcription,* genre is a kind of "sheep's clothing" for Atkinson: the Brodie novels "delight because they are not really about Brodie at all. His investigations, which he performs winningly but without any extraordinary ability or expertise, are mostly just pretexts for exhuming and solving the 'mystery' of the ordinary women's lives at their heart." Dee describes Atkinson's reader friendliness (plot, character, description—in an age when serious literary fiction is often formally defiant) as a kind of "Trojan Horse, a way of delivering something pointed in the guise of something smoothly familiar." Certainly, as we have seen, it is hard to argue with Dee's points. Women's lives are central in Atkinson's fiction, even in the Brodie books. Why else tell us about Amelia Land's sad efforts to lose her virginity in *Case Histories*? Or Kitty Winfield's modeling career in *Started Early, Took My Dog*? In *When Will There Be Good News?*, as reviewers have pointed out, the story is really about the aftermath of trauma, about surviving. Most of its prominent characters—Joanna Hunter, Reggie Chase, Jackson, and others less central, Alison Needler and Julia Land—are survivors of traumatic loss. How they cope is at the book's core. Early in that novel Joanna stresses to Reggie, "the only important thing is love. . . . 'When everything else has gone, Love still remains'" (55), and later Joanna tells Jackson and Reggie after her rescue, "'I don't want this in the baby's life forever,' . . . 'Do you understand? The way I've had it in mine?' and Reggie supposed he must have done because he got rid of the whole crime scene-*pouf!*-just like that" (322). In the aftermath of trauma, Joanna has found a key to happiness and, at the end, shares it with Reggie, who is now staying with her, the baby, and the dog, Sadie.

Structurally, *When Will There Be Good News?* is similar to *One Good Turn:* disparate narrative threads are played out in separate chapters, often ending with cliffhangers that are increasingly intertwined until, at a certain point, the main characters gather. Afterward, the various narratives find resolution, more or less, and coincidence precipitates key plot developments. For instance, Reggie rushes to the site of the train accident, and the second body she comes to is a barely alive man; she performs CPR and administers basic first aid (146–47). Paramedics later tell her, "You gave him a chance" (143, 163). She also finds a postcard from Marlee in the man's pocket; the card is addressed to Jackson Brodie, which is why Reggie later uses him to help her find Joanna Hunter. Later, Jackson and Reggie travel to Hunter's house in the night and, coincidentally, a familiar black Nissan happens to be there, and they follow it to a farmhouse in which the kidnapped Joanna Hunter has just killed two of her captors. Finally, on one of the last pages yet another coincidence is revealed that links Joanna Hunter and Jackson. In both novels, too, Jackson makes similar errors—in *One Good Turn* he heads to Cramond Island although the tide is turning against the direction he expects (he misunderstands a casual warning from two strollers heading the other way [87] and so is cut off from shore); in *When Will There Be Good News?*, he boards the train thinking it is heading to London when, in fact, it is going north (again, an older woman alerts him to this, but he disregards her comment [93]). Both books reveal a final surprise that derives from the single-minded determination of two women—Gloria hired Paul Bradley, and Joanna Hunter purchased a gun from Reggie's brother, Billy, and persuaded Andrew Decker to kill himself with it (Decker had killed her mother, older sister, and baby brother and was recently released from prison). In *When Will There Be Good News?* all the main characters are involved in some way in the train accident. Jackson, badly injured and robbed, is consequently out of the book for the first two-thirds or so, which means the mystery plots are probed by Reggie and the police, especially Louise Monroe. In *One Good Turn,* the opening road accident and its aftermath tie the characters because so many of them are witnesses to what happened. So in a general way, the two books share a great deal, although the narrative arcs of common characters push on toward the subsequent novel.

In this regard, a significant change from *One Good Turn* to *When Will There Be Good News?* is that both Jackson and Louise have gotten married in the interim (Julia, too), but not to each other, although it is clear throughout *Good News* they continue to think fondly, even lovingly, about one another. Despite the admirable qualities of her husband, Louise feels her marriage to be confining and frequently scolds herself, "Bad wife" (e.g., 122, 235) when she thinks about or sees Jackson. Ultimately, she resolves that she will leave her husband in the near future (335). Jackson, on the other hand, is married to a woman named Tessa, who does not actually appear in the novel except in his thoughts. As it turns out, he has fallen victim to a romantic confidence scam. When Jackson ran into an old commanding officer from his military days named Bernie (221), what appeared a chance encounter was actually plotted, for Bernie conspired to introduce Tessa to Jackson at a party, and, knowing a bit about Jackson, she presented herself as everything he would want in a partner. Later, readers will recognize a clue: "At first sight, the people at Bernie's party (sorry, *soirée*) seemed strangely vacuous, as if they'd been hired for the night to play at being festive" (223). Four months after meeting, they were married, which was just two months before the events in the book. (Jackson proposed the day after learning Louise was getting married [215].) But it was all an act—Tessa's family history, her job, her name were all faked, and at the end of the novel Jackson discovers Tessa and Bernie have disappeared and his bank account has been emptied. Jackson, who had previously felt "unmanned" because of all his inherited money, is no longer rich, although a fortunate late deposit from the sale of his French property means he is not destitute. In thinking about his recent marriage, Jackson considers that it was a thing completely out of character for him to do; amusingly, both Josie, his first wife, and Julia independently say, "No, it wasn't" (221). Jackson views marriage as "an ideal state" (but as Josie reminds him, he isn't very good at it), and it is his idealism that causes the usually canny Jackson to fall for a scam. (Consequently, in *Started Early, Took My Dog,* when the narrative turns his way, Jackson is searching for his errant wife [46].) At the end of *When Will There Be Good News?* Jackson is no longer romantically tied to anyone, and Louise is close to divorce. As a parting gesture, Jackson anonymously leaves the gift of a border collie puppy on her doorstep for Christmas, which she, strongly suspecting where it came from, calls "Jackson" (338). Again, when *Started Early, Took My Dog* introduces Jackson, an oblique link with Louise is created in the unintentional acquisition of a dog.

The ending of *Started Early, Took My Dog* leaves us wondering about Jackson and Louise, who is largely absent from the book except when Jackson thinks about her. It is only on the penultimate page that her presence is felt when Jackson's phone rings and he must decide whether he should answer. This is where the narrative leaves off, but it is not the end of the book. Its last page, in a strategy that recalls the closings of *Human Croquet,* is Emily Dickinson's poem beginning, "'Hope' is a thing with feathers—" (350). Enigmatic, as so many of Dickinson's poems are, the poem leaves readers wondering: is it Jackson's hope? Louise's? or ours? *Big Sky* does not pick up the relationship, but its conclusion mirrors the call that ended the earlier novel; that is, Jackson phones Louise, who is not in the novel, hangs up without speaking, but she suspects it was him.

Started Early, Took My Dog builds multiple correspondences among characters so that the entwined plots come to reflect each other. Tracy Waterhouse, a retired police inspector, impulsively takes on the responsibilities of raising a four-year-old girl, Courtney, when she offers 3,000 pounds to Kelly Cross, who had care of Courtney. We never actually find out if Courtney is Kelly Cross's child—Kelly's last words to Tracy as bus doors close are, "But she's not—" (29), and the fact that Tracy receives anonymous phone calls, even after leaving Leeds (where the novel is set) for Paris with new identities for herself and Courtney, is not addressed. Jackson's parallel case, although less consequential, is his impulsive acquisition of a dog from an abusive man who we know was not the dog's "true" owner (44). This unplanned action later proves crucial because the dog saves Jackson's life after he has been beaten, tied, gagged, and thrown into a dumpster: the dog's barking alerts the sanitation crew before they dump the bin. What appeared to be chance, the rescue of the dog, emerges as crucial to Jackson's survival. Also contributing to this sort of doubling is the appearance of a second private investigator, Brian Jackson (another former police officer), who actually describes himself at one point as Jackson Brodie's "alter ego" (294). The shared name causes considerable confusion with mistaken identities imperiling Brodie's life. As it turns out, each is working for one of Clair Braithwaite's children, although that is not recognized or revealed until very late in the book. Jackson Brodie is helping Hope McCallister, living in New Zealand, find her birth origins, and Brian Jackson is helping Michael Braithwaite find his sister. The result in *Started Early, Took My Dog* is a tale of police corruption, conspiracy, and cover-up that raises questions about guilt and the choices made to obtain a better life for children. Atkinson has described the book as "very moral. . . . Ethics are not necessarily to do with being law-abiding. I am very interested in the moral path, doing the right thing" (Fox 2011). Many of the book's questions turn on moral issues, but the fact that Tracy's own insights into the murder of Carol Braithwaite are dismissed raises questions of gender bias among the police, albeit in the mid-1970s, as another point of interest. Fundamentally, no one ever escapes the past, and as the epigraph, "For want of a nail . . ." (the phrase often recurs [e.g., 56, 57, 63, 120, 299]) asserts, all actions, even the smallest, can have major consequences. Barry, another police officer, mistreats his son-in-law, Ivan, who drinks to settle his nerves, then drives off impaired, which results in an accident that kills Barry's infant grandson and leaves his daughter on life support. Now Barry is haunted by his guilt, and his wife, Barbara, sleepwalks through her life. The whole sequence has its origins in what might have been an insignificant matter, when Ivan lost a flash drive with his business's accounts on it between the cushions at Barry's and Barbara's house, but Barry's failure to return it is catastrophic: Ivan's business fails, Ivan asks Barry for a loan, Barry rips in to Ivan, Ivan drinks, etc. (324–25). Small things in the right context lead to disaster.

Tracy's future will be marked by her past as well, and her life will be a haunted one: "Tracy would forever be looking over her shoulder, waiting for the knock on the door" (345). The past is always present, as Jackson well knows: "all this time, in all these places, standing in the bare ruined choirs and the echoing engine sheds or sitting in the tearooms and the Golden Fleece pubs, his sister was there in the shadows, laughing and shaking blossom off her clothes, . . . she had gone before him and he was never going to catch her" (349)—all of which makes Michael Braithwaite's plaintive "Where's my sister?" (347) another echo for the reader.

From its title on, *Started Early, Took My Dog* is marked by lines and phrases from Emily Dickinson's poetry, which often enter Jackson's thoughts because he is drawn to her verse (52–53). (Dickinson also supplies the epigraph for *When Will There Be Good News?*) The final poem in *Started Early, Took My Dog* casts a positive glow over the book: "'Well, only the ending's lovely,' Jackson said, 'not the story itself.' 'A child who is found,' Julia said. 'Isn't that the best thing in the world?' 'What was left in the box,' Jackson said" (317). The final reference here is to the story of Pandora, also referred to a few times in this book: "'Pandora's box,' Julia said, . . . 'Although the word *pithos* actually translates as "large jar." Pandora released evil into the world and—' 'I know,' Jackson interrupted. 'I know what she did.' 'People have a need to find the truth,' Julia said. 'Human nature can't abide a mystery.' In Jackson's experience, finding the truth-whatever that was-only deepened the mystery of what had really happed in the past" (77). Presumably, the story we just read reflects the evil in the world, but hope, "the thing with feathers," remains.

The "literariness" of *Started Early, Took My Dog*'s allusions touches again on the question of genre and the self-reflexive characteristic of the detective story. As in *One Good Turn,* there is a mystery writer in the text, Marilyn Nettles, who contemptuously dismisses her work as "'books for people who can't read': 'They call it "True Noir" . . . "Women in jeopardy," . . . "Very popular."' 'You have to wonder'" (250). Like Canning, she supports herself with writing she demeans. There is also *Collier,* a fictional television series that Julia has role in and that features Tilly, an aging actress struggling with dementia, to offer a point of contrast to the world of the novel while commenting on the book itself. Julia says of the series, "'It's very popular,' . . . 'Great viewing figures.' Real murder was disgusting. And smelly and messy and usually heartbreaking, invariably meaningless, occasionally tedious, but not this neat sanitized narrative. And the victims were often prostitutes dispensable as tissues, both in reality and in fiction" (181). Significantly, the victims in *Started Early, Took My Dog* (Carol Braithwaite, Rachel Hardcastle, and Kelly Cross) are prostitutes, so the novel conforms to its self-defined generic expectations. The text's reflexivity extends to its discourse reminding us of its status as language: "Kill Kelly Cross. Even the alliteration was alluring" (187). Elsewhere, "Jackson was long enough in the tooth to know that it was over when you started reaching for the clichés" (356). Again, language and words are the means by which we construct our worlds: "Reality itself was nothing. Words, everything was made out of words, once you lost the words you lost the world" (309). Tilly realizes she is losing words and, we see, her world. She is being killed off in *Collier,* and Atkinson includes a page or so of the screenplay that we read as Tilly reads it as well: in an odd way, she uncannily experiences her own death. Tilly unwittingly saves Tracy and Courtney but dies in the struggle with Lomax, the retired but corrupt police officer who had killed Carol Braithwaite. Just before her death, Tilly sees "a bad man who wanted to hurt the 'Twinkle, Twinkle' child. For a second she thought she saw her father in his face" (314). The aged actress, her thoughts clouded with lines from Shakespeare saves the "Twinkle, Twinkle girl" from the bad man. Tilly's story is just one of many in Atkinson's oeuvre that could form the basis of a novel. As is the case with Louise Monroe; Sylvie Todd in *Life After Life;* or even Alice, who is partially rescued in *Behind the Scenes at the Museum,* the stories of secondary characters surface in the narratives and then submerge. The appearance of Edward Todd in his own novel demonstrates the vast potential in narrative branches that Atkinson hints at in *Started Early, Took My Dog* but leaves, for obvious reasons, undeveloped: "A family tree was fractal, its branches dividing endlessly" (138). It is enough to know that any story is only a part of an ever-expanding narrative galaxy. Atkinson's fictional universe is unbounded, so in this sense to bracket her books (three developing postmodern novels; five Brodie books; two Todd books or, perhaps, three Second World War books) betrays the logic of her texts.

FIVE

War and Other Things

Life After Life, A God in Ruins, and *Transcription*

Life After Life

After four Jackson Brodie novels, Atkinson's next opens in 1930 with a woman pulling a gun on a man we learn is Hitler, but why would she think he should be killed? As Atkinson says, the would-be assassin would have to have experienced the war (Laws 2013a). And so we embark on *Life After Life,* a book in which Ursula Todd, its central character and possible assassin, is born and dies repeatedly while living different lives but remaining the same character in the same family. *Life After Life* is in many ways the formal culmination of Atkinson's work: here she weaves multiple overlapping narrative strands in a highly allusive novel that ranges over Britain's twentieth century, with the Second World War and especially the Blitz being central to a reexamination of the myths retailed about that history and that war.[1] In this respect, Atkinson participates in the ongoing reconsideration of Britain's past, and especially of the wars, which has been undertaken by several contemporary novelists such as Ian McEwan in *Atonement* and Sarah Waters in *The Night Watch,* who both deal with the Second World War, and Pat Barker in her *Regeneration* trilogy, who looks at the Great War. The very premise of *Life After Life* implies that big questions about free will, destiny, time, and the role of chance will be raised in the mind of the reader. But few, if any, answers will be provided.

At Fox Corner, the name of the family home, Ursula Todd is the middle child of Sylvie and Hugh. Their oldest is Maurice, who is followed by Pamela, then Ursula, Edward (called Teddy), and a bit later a baby brother, Jimmy. Mrs. Glover is the cook, and Bridget is the young Irish housemaid. Hugh's sister, Izzie, also plays important roles in the book. The same is true of Nancy Shawcross, a neighbor with whom Teddy forms a close relationship. One of Nancy's older sisters, Millie, becomes a particular friend of Ursula's, and for a time they share an apartment in the early days of the war. Numerous other characters make appearances, but it is Ursula who dominates the book, with her parents (especially her mother), aunt, and younger brother Teddy being most relevant to its several narrative strands.

Ursula Todd is born repeatedly on February 11, 1910; indeed, she emerges into the world eleven times. In a book where months and years are identified in chapter headings to help locate events in history, "11 February 1910" appears twelve times, with its last occurrence on the final page, telling us that the midwife on her way to attend the birth has been held up at a pub by a snowstorm and so will not be able to get to Fox Corner. It is a circumstance we have already encountered, and the results of this missed appointment in the book's first sections are varied. Initially, in the absence of a doctor and the midwife, both held up by snow, Ursula dies very soon after birth; another time Sylvie cuts the umbilical cord herself, the child is saved; on other occasions the doctor arrives; still later, Sylvie, acting ahead of her time, performs artificial respiration to revive the infant Ursula, who was nearly smothered by a cat. (Dr. Fellowes, like many of fiction's patronizing male doctors, discounts the efficacy of Sylvie's actions, declaring the favorable result coincidental [146].[2]) Readers soon come to understand what is happening. Ursula's life is wholly dependent on small matters of circumstance so that, as Melanie Micir and Rosario Arias both observe, the novel's structuring force, its main premise is "what if?" (Micir 2017, 518; Arias 2015, 125); "History," Ursula's nephew Nigel later says, "is all about 'what ifs'" (427). Or, to recall a trope from *Started Early, Took My Dog,* "for want of a nail."

As the novel moves from 1910 through to the 1960s, Ursula's life and lives occur alongside crucial periods of national making, particularly the Great War, the Spanish influenza, the Second World War, and the Blitz. Consequently, the book has been viewed as a postmodern take on the historical novel, although the particular historical moments it deals with, however profound, are limited in number. Micir sees the novel as "a counterfactual historical novel and counterhistorical feminist fantasy in Woolf's modernist mode" (2017, 525). (Micir links the book to Woolf's "modernist historical novel" *Orlando.*) Notably, Micir observes that women want the chance to rewrite history, to change what happens (2017, 528). The book has also been linked to the tradition of the country house novel, and it is clear that the contrast between the domesticity of Fox Corner and bomb-ravaged London is central to a probing of "Englishness" so often tied to rural continuities, while the 1910 birth date is associated, as Atkinson attests in her "Note from the Author," to E. M. Forster (482), whose *Howard's End* appeared in that year and, perhaps, offered some plot details to Atkinson. For instance, as a teenager, Izzie went to the Continent and had a baby adopted by German parents; in *Howard's End,* Helen Schlegel, when she is pregnant, also travels to Germany to have her baby. Sylvie, early in the book, is said to be reading an early Forster (53) while, in another echo of *Howard's End,* the division of family property following Sylvie's death is described as "all rather Forsterian" (416). Ursula, not wanting to quarrel, takes only Sylvie's "little carriage clock," which Sylvie had hidden from the bailiffs after her father died; the clock is referred to a few times in *Life After Life,* but it also recalls the clock Bunty rescued from her past and the one Pamela takes to Australia in *Behind the Scenes at the Museum.* (Like dogs, the clock is recurring detail in Atkinson's work.) In terms of the historical moments in the book, the general strike of 1926, the economic depression of the 1930s, the postwar Cold War tensions, the Suez crisis, the cultural reemergence of Britain in the 1960s, and the Six-Day War get barely a glance, if that. (The odious Maurice and his friend Howie plan to go up to London during the 1926 strike to drive buses, trains, or what have you "to keep the country running" [185]. Since both are such unpleasant characters, it is hard not to read this as judgment on their conservative politics.)

While Hugh is a veteran of the Great War, in which Izzie also participated, it is Ursula's experiences in the Blitz that are "the dark, beating heart of novel" ("Note From the Author" 482) and get the most space in the text. As *A God in Ruins* and *Transcription* later confirm, the lived experience of the Second World War for individuals most engages Atkinson's interest, not the military or geopolitical concerns. Ursula works in the Home Office but during the raids she is part of an air raid precaution (ARP) team headed by Miss Woolf. Teddy's war experience is more fully described in *A God in Ruins,* but we learn in *Life After Life* that he flew Halifax bombers in the Royal Air Force (RAF), was shot down in 1943, and was presumed dead; in another narrative route, however, he was taken prisoner and survived the war.

In *Life After Life* Ursula slowly develops an inkling of what is going on with her, but that awareness comes over time, and while she does eventually learn something of what she is experiencing, her understanding is far from complete. Although addressed obliquely in conversation with her aunt Izzie, Ursula never overtly discusses the feelings and premonitions she has with anyone except Dr. Kellet, an analyst her mother took her to after Ursula had pushed Bridget down the stairs (158). Kellet becomes a kind of spiritual guide for Ursula, especially in his last appearances in the book, but he cannot really explain Ursula's feelings. After he is retired and in one of her incarnations he says to her, "You are an old soul. . . . It can't be easy. But your life is still ahead of you. It must be lived" (456). Pushing Bridget down the stairs, though, was the result of the young Ursula learning from her experience of other lives: it was her final attempt to prevent the 1918–19 influenza from entering her family's home: "All she knew was that she *had* to do it. The great sense of dread had come over her and she had to do it" (130). It did, however, take a few incarnations for her to learn not only the source of the illness but also how to prevent it from being spread. In other earlier lives, Ursula saw that various family members, including herself, died of the illness. Regarding her pushing Bridget, "Practice makes perfect"—the cliché is a favorite of Sylvie (e.g. 87) and Pamela, Ursula's sister, but the narrator applies it here because Bridget is finally prevented from attending armistice celebrations (129). (In yet another life, we learn she does not attend because she had heard, from Ursula, that her boyfriend, Clarence, who she would have gone with, was seen kissing another woman [445].) Given such knowledge, it is not surprising that Ursula should seem "forlorn all the time" (162), and Sylvie considers Ursula's moods another reason for seeing Dr. Kellet.

Ursula's war experiences dominate in the novel but are only part of her lived experiences. Her narrative arcs move in multiple directions, and in some of them she doesn't live long enough to see the Second World War. There is understandably an urge to see Ursula's incarnations as progressive: the epigraph from Edward implies as much (vii, 405). Does Ursula have the repeated opportunity to correct past mistakes and "to undo the traumatic events that caused her previous death(s)" so as to move toward a full and proper life with things set "right for her and her beloved ones" (Arias 2015, 125)? The temptation to see the book this way, as Rosario Arias does, is strong but, I think, best avoided. As it opens, someone—presumably Ursula, we later infer—attempts to kill Hitler. We have no idea if she is successful in this; the event is narrated as part of one of Ursula's lives that occurs prior to the first account of her birth, but it also appears tied to an incarnation we read about later (461–63). However, we also read about other incarnations that have her visiting Germany to learn German and, in another path, marrying a German man, Jürgen Fuchs, and then finding herself trapped in Germany when the war breaks out. In this latter narrative, Ursula's plans to escape the country are thwarted by circumstance (the British Embassy closes before she can get to it) and by her husband, who is later killed in the war; on the threshold of Germany's defeat in the shattered remains of Berlin, Ursula kills her daughter, Frieda, and herself as Soviet troops advance. In interviews promoting *Life After Life,* Atkinson said of the book's opening, "Maybe, she did kill Hitler. Because I wanted to instill in the book—which I suppose it means instill in the reader . . .—the idea that it never ends, obviously, and it is possible, one of these times, she is going to kill Hitler" (Laws 2013a). The results of a successful assassination are speculated on by Ursula and her nephew, Nigel, which opens the possibility of an alternative history being written, but that is not Atkinson's concern here. What she is interested in is how possibilities can unfold from particular origins.

At another moment in the text, following blood poisoning, the "black bat" nears Ursula but then leaves her so she recovers (194). (The bat, darkness, the feel of snow, and sometimes the glitter of a small toy hare hanging from a pram often recur in the passages noting Ursula's passing.) It is possible within the fractal architecture of her lives that in one incarnation she does die of blood poisoning, in another she survives. The implication is that we are not reading about all of her incarnations, and as the last moments with the midwife make clear, they appear to have no end. Indeed, Atkinson's note following *A God in Ruins* suggests that novel is one of Ursula's unwritten lives (385). Elsewhere, Atkinson stressed, "Every life she acquires something. Every life she becomes more heroic" (Laws 2013a). "Not that she improves herself. I think that she gets stronger and . . . more courageous" (Simon 2013). From a metaphysical perspective, such a situation presents human life as endless—perhaps pointless—repetition (hence the compensatory desire to see these incarnations as leading toward some point of fulfillment); from a narrative perspective, it suggests the endless possibilities of storytelling (so it is fiction about fiction).

In the sequence leading to Bridget's fall down the stairs, Ursula is not inspired to act out of some understanding of the nature of her layered lives, nor is she spared the anguish and suffering of living through these varied existences because she can find comfort in the expectation of repetition with difference. Rather, her actions with Bridget stem from an increasingly strong feeling that Bridget must not attend the celebrations of the armistice. But, as with the opening's December 1930 attempt to kill Hitler, it is only after having experienced particular consequences that Ursula can, in a later incarnation, sense the need to alter circumstances. Hence, the first time we read about November 11, 1918, we learn of Ursula's death from influenza; the second time, Ursula feels "a wave of something horrible . . . , a great dread, as if something truly treacherous was about to happen. The same feeling she had had when she'd followed Pamela into the sea when they were in Cornwall. . . . They had been rescued by a stranger" (97). Later she feels "a sudden pinch of fear in her insides" (100). The next time she felt "inexplicable" panic (111), and, after another failed attempt to keep Bridget at Fox Corner, she tries again and succeeds because she pushes Bridget down the stairs: "Practice makes perfect" (129). In this telling, though, Ursula has been trying to explain to Sylvie her sensations of things being somehow familiar, and Sylvie dismisses Ursula's experiences as "peculiar" and "déjà vu" (127). In another incarnation, however, Bridget doesn't fall down the stairs at all, and it is Ursula's headaches, sleepwalking, and her sensations of déjà vu that prompt Sylvie to take Ursula to Dr. Kellet (446–47).

Ursula is perplexed by sometimes knowing what people will say or what will happen, but she learns that these are things best not expressed, so when Pamela wonders what the new neighbors' girls are called, Ursula who already knows says nothing: "She was getting as good at keeping secrets as Sylvie" (129). Later, Creighton, her "man from the Admiralty," suggests that Ursula "would make a good spy" (245) (which, in Atkinson's fiction, puts Ursula in the company of

Tatiana from *One Good Turn* and Juliet Armstrong from *Transcription*). Although they are uncomfortable and often terrifying, Ursula comes to trust her sensations without understanding their origins. So, for example, feeling "her heart knocking in her chest, a sudden familiar but long-forgotten terror triggered" (235), she quickly moves to find Nancy, who has gone to pick berries in a laneway, which prevents Nancy's murder (235); she recognizes danger in Howie, Maurice's friend (231); and she avoids particular situations during the Blitz. For example, she rescues a dog she names "Lucky," but in one life a wall collapses on her, so her having not gone in the shelter, where she knows she would have been killed, means death in another way; later she rescues the dog again but stays back from the falling wall (396–97).

But Ursula's imperfect consciousness of other lives also causes her immense suffering. In a late, disorienting section—for readers and for Ursula—"The End of the Beginning," she experiences her various existences bleeding into each other so that she no longer knows what is real and what isn't (this occasionally happened to her during the Blitz, but Ursula considered it the result of a lack of sleep [391]) and is plagued by guilt and the awareness of things done or not done that altered the course of lives. For example, she blames herself for Nancy's murder (454). The section provides snippets and glimpses in short segments that refer to lives we have already read about and to lives that we have not read about. For readers, the result is confusing because sudden changes have occurred, and the familiar practice of dating events by month and year has been abandoned. For instance, one of the Todd children at the age of four does drown, and Mr. Winton, who much earlier in the book had saved Ursula and Pamela (45), unsuccessfully tried to save the child, but this time it wasn't Ursula or Pamela but, rather, a younger cousin—the boy is Izzie's child who was born at Fox Corner rather than in Germany[3]—named Roland (442). Ursula and Pamela were intent on building a sandcastle and had not noticed the boy's disappearance. For Ursula, what once was able to help her has become a cacophony of experience that precipitates a breakdown, a further, cryptic conversation with Dr. Kellet, and ultimately a kind of acceptance.[4]

There is no grand theory to explain Ursula's experiences presented by either her or the narrator, no metaphysical framing to propose reincarnation, although Dr. Kellet suggests it (157, 160), but much later Ursula suggests that time is like a "palimpsest" (456). And, as far as we know, Ursula is unique in this sort of experience, or perhaps she is unique in being conscious of it; one wonders if what happens with Ursula is true for others (indeed, it must be). Certainly that idea is implied at the end of *A God in Ruins,* but even in *Life After Life* there is the example of Sylvie who in the penultimate "11 February 1910" section is alone with Bridget when Ursula is born blue because of the cord around her neck.

Sylvie rummages furiously in a bedside drawer and finds a pair of surgical scissors: "'One must be prepared,' she muttered. 'Hold the baby close to the lamp so I can see. Quickly, Bridget. There's no time to waste.' Snip, snip. Practice makes perfect" (468). What is peculiar here, and hinted in the final line, is that Sylvie was prepared because of prior experience, and, indeed, in the book's second telling of "11 February 1910" Dr. Fellowes arrives to save Ursula with a pair of surgical scissors: "'Snip, snip,' he said. Sylvie made a mental note, a small, vague one, given her exhaustion and the circumstances of it, to buy just such a pair of scissors, in case of similar emergency. (Unlikely, it was true.)" (21). All lives are altered by the smallest of circumstances: in one case Nancy is murdered, in another she walks home with Ursula; a farmer is killed by a bull, but sometimes Dr. Fellowes is called to attend him and the man lives. In the case of Sylvie, one might wonder how conscious she is of repeated lives. Significantly, it is Sylvie who chooses to send Ursula to Dr. Kellet. Does Sylvie know what Ursula is experiencing? Does she experience it herself? Again, her own life moves along different paths as *A God in Ruins* suggests. In one, grief stricken at the loss of Teddy in the war, she commits suicide on V-E day (*Life After Life*, 136; 415); in another, she lives well after the war and dies of a stroke in the 1950.

A recognized challenge for Atkinson in the book was keeping things "vague enough so that [Ursula] doesn't really understand what's happening" (Laws 2013a). It is the challenge of the historical novelist—to represent the confusion among those in the past about the future. That is, a character in the past, unlike the reader, cannot know the future and so has to act according to her available understanding. Ursula gains a sense of what the future might bring, but even she cannot know what might happen if a particular action, such as killing Hitler, occurs. Would the twentieth century be different? Ursula speculates with her friend Ralph and then later her nephew Nigel on the matter. With Ralph she wonders what would have happened if Hitler had been kidnapped as a child and brought up differently. Ralph responds, "'Nobody knew what was going to happen. And anyway he might have turned out just the same, . . . You might have to kill him instead of kidnapping him. Could you do that? Could you kill a baby?' . . . If I thought it would save Teddy, Ursula thought. Not just Teddy, of course, the rest of the world, too" (261). With Nigel, who is a history tutor at Brasenose College, Oxford, Ursula presents a fuller speculation on how things might have been different had Hitler been killed but concludes as Ralph did, "Perhaps Goering or Himmler would have stepped in. And everything would have happened in just the same way" (428). The question is one of history's great "what if's," which, Nigel says, is what history is all about (427). But this particular question also lies at the origin of Atkinson's novel: "It's always difficult to point to origin of a book. . . . I actually wanted to write a novel about what would have happened if Hitler had been kidnapped as a baby. The nugget of that idea is in the book. And it was sort of a nature/nurture argument" (Laws 2013a). Obviously, the book became more than "this germ of an idea."

As readers we are quickly taught to understand Ursula's life after life, and after a few scenes of her dying, we come to read events from a detached and ironical perspective. The trick for Atkinson, then, is to keep us invested in each of Ursula's lives even as we realize any death she experiences is not the end. In a sense, we are assured that whatever happens will be okay: Ursula, the character we follow, will come back. Theoretically, the book is endless. February 11, 1910, can always return, and another thread can always be spun.

It is to Atkinson's credit that we are invested in each life so Ursula's deaths for the most part do not lose emotional power. We can be distressed by her childhood deaths (at birth, drowning, a fall from an icy roof, influenza) and horrified by her murder at the hands of an abusive husband and by, especially, her suicide in Berlin. In some ways, the book is a collection of stories, each featuring the same character experiencing an alternative life; Melanie Micir describes the book as an "anthology of experiences open to a relatively average English woman in the early twentieth century" (535). Again, the difference is that Ursula feels these past stories and is reminded of them at particular moments. Time, she says, isn't illustrated by the aurabora, usually depicted as a serpent with its tail in its mouth, with its implied notion of cyclic recurrence; rather, she says, it is a palimpsest with the past showing through into the present (456). The narratives do not present history as repetition but as potentialities that are fractally related. As chaos science, popularly recognized since the 1980s in several books such as James Gleick's *Chaos: Making a New Science,* anticipates, small variants in an original state's measurement or circumstance can have huge consequences over time to produce completely different results. *Life After Life* is structured fractally as each "life" of Ursula proceeds from a common origin but minute variance initiates a completely different path. Obviously, there are practical issues that limit the pursuit of this thinking in a novel, for as Ursula gets older the moments that open potential narrative paths multiply. Consequently, it is easiest to present variance in the young Ursula's life: even the account of her birth is shown in four or five ways with the chance event of the snowstorm participating in all. Ursula "dies" more often in the book's first part than in the latter, but I do not think we can say that this is because she takes action to avoid fatal outcomes (the influenza sequence not withstanding). Atkinson surely recognizes the difficulty she has set for herself; that is, the almost infinite opportunities for change that are possible in the course of a life mean that Ursula might never advance beyond childhood if Atkinson had continued as she had been doing.

One way she addresses the problem is by establishing a facile but emotionally powerful cause/effect chain that leads from Ursula's rape to her murder.

The sequence is horrifying in its determinism, but on reflection we see that this somewhat predictable narrative sequence (rape, abortion, maternal rejection, low self-esteem, leaving school, menial work, drinking, marriage to an abuser, murder) is open to other variations in many places. For example, Ursula seems to address in another life the problem of the onanistic secretarial college instructor, Mr. Carver, who initially asks his students to type while blindfolded, at which point he masturbates before them unseen (201). In another life, Ursula, "suspecting there was more to it than monitoring their skills," leads class opposition to the blindfold: "'You're such a rebel,' one of them—Monica—said, admiringly. 'Well, not really,' Ursula said. 'Just being sensible, you know'" (241). Much later we read that Mr. Carver had been arrested for exposing himself (394). So even the most deterministic of narrative sequences offers space for alternatives. That is, Ursula's enrolment in a secretarial college, instead of a university, is initially presented as part of the sequence of events following her rape (199–201), but the fact that she addresses the situation of the instructor implies that she is enrolled there in other incarnations. Similarly, she survives blood poisoning following the abortion, but that certainly need not have happened. She very nearly dies, but she could just as easily not have suffered the illness. Still, her recovery provides the opportunity for a touching scene with her father, Hugh. And Teddy, presumably in another narrative, could have saved her life when confronted with Derek Oliphant's violence. Teddy's own life after Nancy's murder, it is suggested, followed a trajectory of despair similar to Ursula's following her rape and abortion. That is, Ursula's rape is an originary trauma that initiates a life of suffering and early death for her. It becomes the explanation for all the misfortune that follows in that narrative arc. Distraught because of her pregnancy, Ursula boards the train for London, where she eventually seeks her aunt. Meanwhile, Nancy goes missing and, with her death, Ursula's friendship with Millie slowly ends. In Teddy's case, Nancy's murder is equally traumatic and his promising future is derailed—at least in that narrative. In another, however, Ursula's feelings of terror prompt her to leave the station to find Nancy in the lane, and the two walk home together, passing a ragged man along the way.[5] Nancy isn't killed and Teddy's life avoids the arc of despair.

To suggest that a single traumatic event leads to all the suffering that follows is difficult to credit when we consider the national and personal trauma of the Blitz. Indeed, the very stoicism of life in the Blitz implies the ability to overcome trauma, at least on a national level. In Ursula's case, her resilience depends on her taking lessons from a prior existence and applying them in a new life: in a different narrative a swift punch and kick prevents her rape as a teenager. The tale of the Blitz is, as Scott Simon (2013) remarked during an interview with Atkinson on NPR, Britain's *Odyssey* and its *Iliad.* Atkinson responded by acknowledging the immense amount of propaganda that saturates accounts of the

Blitz (see also Magwood 2018), but she also praised the intensity of the period and the stoicism she found in firsthand accounts: "If I could choose a period to go back to, I think I would like to live through the Blitz." It is the Blitz, she notes, in an echo of Ursula's own words (405), that is "the dark, beating heart of the novel" ("Note from Author" 482). In this regard, Atkinson "bears witness" to the history: "'We cannot turn away,' Miss Woolf told her [Ursula], 'we must get on with our job and we must bear witness.' What did that mean, Ursula wondered. 'It means,' Miss Woolf said, 'that we must remember these people when we are safely in the future'" (357). For Atkinson, Miss Woolf is "the moral centre of the Blitz chapters" (483) so it is not surprising to find that Ursula has immense respect for Miss Woolf, who epitomizes the stoical endurance of civilians during the Blitz. Ursula learns from Miss Woolf and comes to share her views on the importance of bearing witness (e.g., 368). As Melanie Micir notes, the name "Woolf" is provocative (2017, 518), even suggesting another alternate history for the novelist, whose London house had been bombed.

Late in the novel we read Ursula "had grown very morbid since Argyll Road. It had affected her in a different way to other incidents" (408). "Argyll Road" here refers to a particular blast in "November 1940" that destroyed the house where, in some incarnations, Ursula lived.[6] Epitomizing the relentless and repeated destruction of the German bombing campaign, the destruction here is told numerous times with Ursula's death in the cellar shelter being part of at least three tellings. Each narrative of the experience opens with the crescent moon (250, 263, 297, 387) and thoughts of poetry (lines are quoted). The narratives also include particular individuals, such as Renee Miller, and particular details, such as Lavinia Nesbit's dress hanging in the stairwell after the blast. In its first telling, Ursula is in the cellar when the bomb hits and survives only a few moments after rescuers (one of whom calls her "Susie") reach her (269–70). Something similar occurs in the second iteration (again she is referred to as "Susie"; 291–92). In a third, rather than die "like a fox in a hole" (387), she chooses not to go into the shelter and notices a dog cowering in a doorway opposite. She reaches the dog as the house is blasted, and momentarily considers herself lucky—only to be killed by a collapsing wall (299). In the fourth, Ursula lives with Millie, who has become an actress but as a member of ARP attends the bombed house on Argyll Road with Mr. Emslie, who calls all the women he comes upon in the bomb wreckage "Susie" in honor of a daughter who died when young of diphtheria (392). Ursula also finds the dog, "Lucky." "November 1940" tells the same story of Argyll Road four times, but each is slightly different. Significantly, the first three tellings are in three different sections of the book that bear the same title, "A Lovely Day Tomorrow." The fourth "November 1940" is part of "A Long Hard War" and, because Ursula survives, continues with further months and years. It is not surprising, then, that Ursula should be affected differently by the Argyll Road bombing, which unconsciously resonates for her. The incident is a repeated trauma. Between the final "A Lovely Day Tomorrow" and "A Long Hard War" is a section called "The Land of Begin Again" that tells of Ursula's life in Germany and her last days in Berlin. Her experience here allows for some uncanny moments in later sections (386, 429).

The novel's sections that recount life during the Blitz are particularly detailed both in how they describe people's efforts to retain some sense of normalcy and in their descriptions of the gruesome task of searching for survivors among the rubble. For instance, Ursula has romantic relationships with Ralph, from her German language class, and with, more significantly, Alexander Creighton, a married "man from the Admiralty," while the group from Ursula's ARP station develops into a small community which is a microcosm of civilian society. At one point, Miss Woolf, the leader, urges the capable members of the team, some of whom are professionals, to present a small musical concert. Mr. Armitage, an opera singer, performs pieces by Mozart and Puccini to Miss Woolf's piano accompaniment while Herr Zimmerman, a refugee violinist, plays a piece by Bach (385–86). These moments, similar to the concert Ursula and Teddy attend in *A God in Ruins,* emphasize the persistence of art and beauty despite the war's destruction; as Miss Woolf whispers, "Great beauty transcends all" (386). Similarly, the poetry Ursula thinks of prior to the bombing at Argyll Road (by Shakespeare, Keats, Vaughn, Donne, Marvell, to name a few) provide a sharp contrast to the barbarity of the war. The music, it seems, and Miss Woolf notes how much is German, hints at the absurd gap between Germany and Britain; art transcends nationalism and martial conflict.

This high-minded cultural expression is set against the often gruesome descriptions of Ursula's experience, the horrors of which overwhelm even the most inured on occasion: Ursula "vomited after nearly every incident. Mr. Armitage and Mr. Palmer too, Mr. Simms before. Only Miss Woolf and Mr. Bullock seemed to have strong stomachs for death" (358). But even Miss Woolf is temporarily broken by the death of Anthony, a messenger boy, "'Oh, God,' Miss Woolf cried. 'I can't bear it.' 'But bear it we must,' Ursula said, . . . thinking how once this exchange would have been the other way round" (397), and the death, earlier, of Mr. Palmer who had been part of the team: "then she realized that Miss Woolf was very upset. 'It's different when you know someone,' she said. . . . Ursula couldn't find a pulse. 'Shall we move him?' she said. She took his shoulders and Miss Woolf his ankles and Mr. Palmer's body came apart like a Christmas cracker" (377). Although the tone of the last simile seems a bit cool, it points to the unflinching nature of these descriptions of the Blitz: Ursula crawling headfirst into wreckage feeling for bodies (359), bodies and parts of bodies shoveled up in the street (357), and then the things Ursula does not mention at Fox Corner, "wading in effluent from ruptured pipes . . . the gruesome sensation of putting your hand on a man's chest and finding that your hand had somehow slipped *inside* that chest" (365). Ursula survives in the last telling of November 1940, but May 1941 reveals that her post received a direct hit, killing Herr Zimmerman, who played the violin, and Mr. Simms (407). Fred Smith—the butcher's boy from home, now a firefighter who Ursula had a short relationship with—is killed in the same raid. Teddy is shot down in November 1943. And in the February 1947 section of "A Long Hard War" we read that Miss Woolf died in late June 1944 in the Aldwych rocket attack. Ursula's friend Anne, who worked in the Air Ministry, was also killed then (422) and so did not meet Ursula for lunch to tell her something. Ursula wonders if Anne's news would have had to do with Teddy—and, given the book's penultimate part, "May 1945," that is a possibility, but, then, everything in the novel is a possibility.

We can easily get lost in the mirroring in *Life After Life* and ponder the questions of destiny, free will, and relations between cause and effect. Atkinson has set a real challenge for herself—why are any of the lives of Ursula that we read the only ones that we do read? Clearly there must be others, and is her last death really the end? The book does, of course, return us to the midwife and the snowstorm in language that repeats a much earlier telling of February 11, 1910 (477, 146–47). Yet there is the hint that not all deaths are morally equal. Most movingly, the deaths of Ursula and her daughter in Berlin near the war's end are clearly a moment apart: "She had never chosen death over life before and as she was leaving she knew something had cracked and broken and the order of things had changed. Then the dark obliterated all thoughts" (348). What, we might wonder, is "the order of things"?

In narrating that moment in this way, Atkinson not only presents the consequences of aerial bombardment from the other side but she also deftly evades the possible danger that readers detach from Ursula and so become inured to her various ends. As Francine Prose (2013) and Sarah Lyall (2013) noted in separate reviews, we remain invested in each narrative strand, which is crucial to the book's artistry and to its achievement. Unlike the hyper self-consciousness of Italo Calvino's *If on a Winter's Night a Traveller,* also cited by Lyall, which discourages readers from an emotional tie to the narrating voice because we are cerebrally engaged in a meditation on reading, on authorship, and on books as literature and as objects, Atkinson's narration retains a lyrically engaging quality, combined with a sharp sense of realism and history, that compels our attachment to each of Ursula's narrative paths. Reading *Life After Life,* as Lyall again notes, is a bit like reading Ian McEwan's *Atonement,* another novel that contrasts a country house setting with the catastrophe of the war. We do not become inured to the death of "the character" in *Life After Life*, but we do come to know that there is a kind of comfort to be found in the knowledge that any one death is not the end of Ursula. Hence, it may come as a relief to find a new beginning after the horrors of her murder or of Berlin or of some of the Blitz sequence, particularly the Argyll Road bombing. On the other hand, the repetition of our discovery of the what we learn is horrific intensifies our feelings of dread that recur seemingly without end—as the bombings must have seemed to those who endured them night after night, never knowing how things would be different the next time around.

What Atkinson achieves is presenting the reader with an ironical vision that, in many ways and on many levels, comes to mirror Ursula's own experience. Characters say and do things in one life that resonate elsewhere because they are relevant in a different way there: "'Ironic, one might say,' Sylvie said, 'for Clarence to have survived the war and to die of an illness.' ('What would I have done if one of you had caught the influenza?' she often said.)" (168). Similarly, Sylvie says to Ursula at one point, "I'm always so glad . . . that I don't have to take a turn at being other people" (250). Sylvie's comments are registered as ironical by readers who are familiar with Ursula's recurring situation. (Similarly, Ursula's occasional comments on life being random or being singular in *A God in Ruins* [108] resonate differently for readers who know *Life After Life.*) We are, in a sense, rereading even as we read, but the text is never quite the same. Like Ursula, we have memories of what has come before. The net effect is to place us in a position analogous to Ursula's; like her, we sense what will or could happen. Time may be a palimpsest but so is the narrative.

Elsewhere in Atkinson's fiction, it is a second reading that releases the irony we were not aware of the first time (Ruby remarks early in *Behind the Scenes at the Museum* that she feels crowded in the womb but it is only after the book's end that we understand that remark as indicative of her twin sister's presence), and we are enticed in *Behind the Scenes at the Museum* and in *Life After Life* to reread the books: *Behind the Scenes at the Museum* for the marks of ellipsis, repression, and evasion; *Life After Life* because the book returns to its opening —February 11, 1910. Putting the reader in a position analogous to Ursula's is disorienting but ultimately helps us invest in each life and care about the outcome. Again, Atkinson is treading on a fine edge: why should we care when Ursula's life goes badly? After all, we can find our fairy-tale satisfaction in another narrative arc. Ursula put great faith in "the restoration of justice" that fairy-tale endings offered (335), while Atkinson has commented that she is drawn to fairy-tale endings: "it would be very hard for me, as a writer, to give a bad ending to a good character, or give a good ending to a bad character" (Lyall 2013). Obviously, though, the attention to historical detail and realism work against a fairy tale's reassurance. Still, there is a tension in the book that is harder to locate. In some places in *Life After Life* we still get the coolly detached and witty narrative voice that was more often present in Atkinson's first three novels.

This tone can sometimes seem at odds with events, so there is the risk of diminishing the emotional impact of those and future occurrences. Ursula's repeated attempts to evade fate when she and her household suffer the devastations of the influenza become almost ghoulishly funny: "Darkness soon fell again" (112), or, more to my point, "Darkness, and so on" (119). The next, last?, attempt succeeds and the moment ends with the detachment of "Practice makes perfect" (129). The same imagery in other places is lyrically evocative of Ursula's final moments, whether in calm acceptance or in the horror of violence (domestic or martial). One senses a postmodern self-awareness, its attendant reflexivity, bumping against a narrative tradition that builds character, context, and consciousness, and that explores a historically changing world of fading class distinctions, declining national prestige, and war. The dichotomy is crudely analogous to the differences between Atkinson's first three novels and the Brodie books. *Life After Life* shows the two strains coexisting. In *A God in Ruins,* the distinction is explicitly debunked as "a false divide," but what is clear is that Atkinson, as an author saturated in the practice and theory of postmodern fiction, cannot pretend that language and fiction are transparent: the challenge is to express an informed literary sensibility, and so unite the writer who wrote a doctoral dissertation with the person who writes fiction. *Life After Life* represents the culmination of this project. Tellingly, both Todd books include an afterword with Atkinson analyzing her own texts.

As Francine Prose (2013) suggests, *Life After Life* is "as much about writing as it is about anything else." Noting an impressive but partial list of writers that Atkinson alludes to, Prose quips that the book could provide a useful bibliography. In fact, the book has its own bibliography in "A Note from the Author," where Atkinson tells us the book, if she is pressed to say, is "about being English," which, "on reflection, perhaps that's what all my books are about" (483), which is as true as Prose saying it is about writing. "Fiction is fiction, after all" (484), Atkinson adds. But it is notable that the supplied bibliography is entirely tied to the war and especially the Blitz. Derrida may have claimed there is nothing outside the text—*il n'y a pas de hors-texte* (often cited as justification for postmodern playfulness)—but what he meant was that the text, language, is all one has as a means of understanding what language cannot master. Atkinson, realizing the gravity of particular subjects, curtails textual and narrative flippancy so we can understand something of their impact. This situation may in some respects explain particular tonal differences in *Life After Life.* It is one thing to have a child's attempts to prevent Bridget from attending victory celebrations in 1918 told in an increasingly perfunctory manner, but it may be another to be flippant about, say, the Argyll Road bombing and the recurring image of Lavinia Nesbit's dress hanging above a stairwell (it is actually her body). Obviously, the war and especially the Blitz continue to shape the nation's narrative of itself and of the community that highlights virtues of resilience and endurance. One can acknowledge the mythic aspects of the Blitz or Dunkirk or, in the years since, British efforts to crack the German "enigma" code, and recognize how these events were used in wartime propaganda, but lived reality defies the deconstructionist and the skeptic.[7] Hence, Atkinson's bibliography demands that we take things seriously, so we cannot just dismiss Ursula's endings in the Blitz, or elsewhere, as play to be redressed a few pages later. *Life After Life* may present an "anthology" of women's experiences in the early twentieth century, but it also "bears witness" to a traumatic and formative history.

A God in Ruins

A "'companion' piece rather than a sequel" to *Life After Life* ("Author's Note," 385), *A God in Ruins* focuses on Edward Todd (Teddy) and often refers to events and characters who were presented in the earlier book. *A God in Ruins* is quite a different text, though, and while containing some of Atkinson's consistent themes (the absence of the good mother, for example, seen in his daughter Viola's haphazard neglect of her children), the book's narrative movement is smoother, although the chronology changes as Teddy's thoughts drift. *Life After Life* gave us different narrative arcs as Ursula moved in different lives that ended in varied ways. *A God in Ruins* works from *Life After Life*'s last arc—Ursula's final death from a stroke the June 1967—to present Teddy's life during the war, with Nancy, with Viola, and with his grandchildren Sunny and Bertie. Viola's life is present in chapters devoted to it, but most of the past is told through Teddy's thoughts and memories. Atkinson ranges freely there, so much of what happens in the book is forecast well in advance—which does not mean there are no surprises. Sometimes, too, Teddy's memories are contrasted with other versions of the same events, so we do have a kind of repetition with difference, but certainly the transitions are less jarring than in *Life After Life,* and his view remains dominant.

Teddy's future is revealed in proleptic asides and, of course, in the sections dealing with Viola and his grandchildren. When we do reach the point at which particular events are narrated, Nancy's death, for example, it is viewed as something that has already happened. Again there is an ironic perspective in *A God in Ruins,* as in *Life After Life,* but it works in a slightly different fashion, although it is still dependent on a conception of narrative time that is far from linear. The surprise comes in the specifics. In the case of Nancy's death (she has an inoperable brain tumor), Teddy ultimately fulfills her request to assist in her death (307), but because he initially refused her (301–2), readers are not prepared for it nor are we prepared for the fact that Viola had seen him smother Nancy. He is, though, deeply distressed by his action, and it is only the coaxing of Nancy's attendant physician that prevents Teddy from turning himself in (305–6). But even here there is an irony because Dr. Webster assumed Teddy had used morphine (307); indeed, Webster made sure there was enough on hand for this purpose (306).

In the "Author's Note," Atkinson offers the idea that the book is about the fall from grace (numerous references from a portrait of Sylvie painted by her father—"Look mournful . . . think of the Fall of Man" [21]—to poetry, especially to William Blake's "The Sick Rose" and Gerard Manley Hopkins's "Spring and Fall," carry the notion throughout). Although Teddy is kind and loving, as a bomber pilot and as a husband and father, his actions are fraught with moral complexity. Crucially, Viola's witnessing of Teddy's role in Nancy's death is something she keeps secret from him, just as he never confesses that role to her. The result is a gulf between father and daughter that is never bridged, but for readers this central trauma becomes a convenient explanation for Viola's behavior toward her children, her father, and herself. Presumably, she has shared the moment with her analyst—"Everyone liked her father. He was good. He was kind. She had watched him kill her mother" (329)—but it is unclear whether such an obvious trauma could explain all of Viola's anger. Viola's anger, however, while important in the narrative of her redemption, is dwarfed by those parts dealing with Teddy's military service, especially the three episodes recounting the bombings of Turino, Hamburg, and Nuremburg. Two of these involve him witnessing the deaths of friends, Vic and then Keith, and on the third, over Nuremburg, his plane is shot down. For each of these, and other cases, Teddy keeps the experiences to himself, although he does share some details of the war with Sunny and Bertie at different times. Viola has little interest in Teddy's war except to challenge the morality of his actions. Later she regrets not asking about the war, yet her interest is typically framed as self-interest: "She wished she had asked him about his war when he was still *compos mentis.* She might have been able to use his memories as the basis of a novel. . . . People always took war novels seriously" (316).

This last comment touches on the reflexive nature of *Life After Life* and *A God in Ruins.* Indeed, in her interview with Fiona Tolan in 2006, Atkinson confronted the sexism of the critical establishment: "There's a sense that women write about more frivolous things. Which isn't true. . . . But you do have to write about the war to be taken seriously. And also humour is very doubtful I think" (Tolan 2008, 5). Viola is hardly a cipher for Atkinson, but in this respect Atkinson uses Viola to address indirectly many of the issues that affected the reception of her own work while also having a bit of fun. Her first "war novel," though obviously more than that, *Life After Life,* followed four crime novels that often resulted in questions about genre writing being put to her. Viola, late in *A God in Ruins,* is scheduled to speak at a conference in Singapore: "she was down for a couple of panel events. . . . 'The role of the writer in the contemporary world.' 'Popular versus literary-a false divide?' Something like that. It was always something like that" (332). Viola has become a successful popular novelist with many devoted readers "(almost exclusively women)," but she has an uncertain critical reputation that she would like to improve, perhaps by writing "a different kind of book" under a pseudonym (311). One of her books, *Exile from Love,* is praised in *Woman's Own* as "A poignant tale of struggle and loss"; *Good Housekeeping* calls her last novel "her best yet" (307), and another source, *Mumsnet,* judges her "Almost as good as Jodi Picoult" (322).[8] Viola's fiction is popular, but Atkinson's joke is that the very places that praise it are the places that first published her own work.[9] Consequently, while these comments on Viola's fiction offer gentle mocking, given what we know of Viola, they also point to the very critical divide that Atkinson sees as tinged with sexism. Viola does aspire to significant fiction. "'The true nightmares occur when we are awake,' according to the narrator of *Every Third Thought,* her last novel" (307), and we are meant to catch this as referring to Viola's childhood trauma—her mother's death at the hands of her father.[10]

Viola is often treated ambivalently and ironically: at once praised for her romance novels by women's magazines (322), she is revealed in the text as selfish and unloving, until near the book's end. However, the nature of the story as a story is more apparent in the small occasional comments from the narrator-storyteller. As we have seen in discussing her earlier work, Atkinson sees all fiction as being in some measure about fiction ("Author's Note," 387). In this regard we find ourselves in a quandary at the book's end that recalls the earlier work, especially *Human Croquet,* and perhaps reminds us of Ian McEwan's ending for *Atonement.* That is, the chapter describing Teddy's dying ("2012 The Last Flight Dharma" [364–74]) presents the collapse of the house of fiction and offers an almost lyrical summation of details and images that have been present throughout. His dying is metaphorically described as the crumbling of temple walls, while his thoughts drift back to his burning plane over Nuremburg. And then:

> And with a massive roar the fifth wall comes down and the house of fiction falls, taking Viola and Sunny and Bertie with it. They melt into thin air and disappear. Pouf!
>
> The books Viola wrote vanish from bookshelves as if by magic. . . . Nancy marries a barrister in 1950 and has two sons. During a routine examination, her brain cancer is discovered and successfully removed. . . .
>
> A man standing on Westminster Bridge turns away after the Jubilee barge, *Gloriana* has passed beneath the bridge. For a moment he thinks

> someone is standing beside him but there is no one there only a fluctuation in the air. He feels as if he has lost something but can't imagine what it might be. . . . Sylvie overdoses on sleeping tablets on VE Day, unable to come to terms with a future that doesn't contain Teddy, her best boy.
>
> Across the world millions of lives are altered by the absence of the dead, but three members of Teddy's last crew . . . all marry and have children, fractals of the future.
>
> Fifty-five thousand, five hundred and seventy-three dead from Bomber command. . . . And so on and so on and so on, all the way back to the Garden when Cain killed Abel. (373–74)

The whole of this final sequence puts us back into the realm of other, alternative lives that *Life After Life* exploited. Indeed, Sylvie's suicide is a possibility told in the earlier novel (415), although in *A God in Ruins* we earlier learned that she died of a stroke in the late 1950s (174). In the chapter following the house of fiction's collapse, "1947 Daughters of Elysium," Nancy and Ursula watch a skylark, one of the book's early images (12), and Nancy imagines it to be a reincarnated Teddy: Ursula responds, somewhat ironically if we know *Life After Life,* "I believe we have just one life, and I believe that Teddy lived his perfectly" (*God in Ruins* 376). Her comment reflects back on one of the epigraphs in *Life After Life.* Still, *A God in Ruins* does not end with the brief "Daughter of Elysium" chapter; following, "And when all else is gone, Art remains. Even Augustus" (376), several pages of an Augustus adventure unfold that pick up from much earlier in *A God in Ruins* when Ursula is reading aloud to Teddy (40). Pained, the young Teddy urges her to "please stop reading now" (384). The "Author's Note" follows, so the command to "stop reading now" signals an end to the Todd narrative but not necessarily the book.

How are we to think of these multiplying conclusions? In *Human Croquet,* Isobel wakes on her sixteenth birthday and the narrative ensues, but at the book's end we learn she has been unconscious since a tree fell on her. Everything we have read has been imaginary (which accounts in large measure for the narrative's fantastical elements, including its playing with time). In *A God in Ruins,* time is presented as fluid within the storytelling, but this narrative, excepting Teddy's final pages, lacks the fantastical elements that *Human Croquet* exploits.[11] Only in the chapter that discusses Sunny's stay at Jordan Manor ("1982 The Courage of the Small Hours") do we encounter description that evokes, in this case, fairy tale with the now abandoned Sunny at the mercy of cruel grandparents and nasty "servants" in a gothic wasteland that Teddy likens to Miss Havisham's abode in *Great Expectations* (249). For Sunny the stay proves traumatic in that not only is he treated badly but his erratic father, in a drug-induced haze, nearly has him killed along with himself, while staring at an oncoming train. Sunny frees himself but witnesses Dominic's death. Then, in a situation that recalls Ruby Lennox's trauma stemming from Pearl's death, his grandparents blame him for his father's death because an inquest and media reports suggest Dominic was trying to save Sunny from the train and so the father died a "hero." Sunny will never learn the truth of what happened, we are told (247) (unlike Ruby), but he is obviously traumatized, as indicated by his bed-wetting, although his grandmother believes Sunny should "get on with things as if nothing had happened" (245). (The cruelties inflicted upon children is another consistent theme in Atkinson's work.) There is no real happy ending to this part of the tale, although Teddy and Bertie rescue a grateful Sunny.

The fairy-tale aspects of Jordan Manor and the narrative puzzles of the book's ending are contrasted by the detailed and convincing accounts of Teddy's war experience. As in *Life After Life,* the reality of the war overwhelms textual play. Indeed, details that might be more suited to macabre or "ghoulish" (113, 146) fantasy are present as simple fact: Hilda, a Women's Auxilary Air Force member at Teddy's airbase, is decapitated by a propeller blade sheering from a damaged plane—Teddy "went out and picked up the head" (147–48); in *Life After Life,* the body of Mr. Palmer comes "apart like a Christmas cracker" when Ursula and Miss Woolf pick it up (377). Neither Teddy nor Ursula become inured to the horror they experience: Ursula vomits after every incident (*Life* 358), and Teddy is lost in the memory of Hilda's death when out with Sunny (147). Ursula in *Life After Life* experiences the war several times but in different ways; Teddy relives his experiences through random memories stirred by conversation, an object, or, explicitly, the "farewell tour" he takes with Bertie in 1999. For Teddy, life after the war is a life he never expected to have. The war is such a defining event for him that life in the afterward can seem boring, even "plodding" in Nancy's view (169, 182, 287). As several reviewers observed, Teddy's youthful promise has hardly been fulfilled. He does not travel (which Viola reproaches him for [210]), and he doesn't challenge himself creatively. At one time, before the war, he aspired to write poetry or a novel, but he failed at those (86, 89) and what he does write—his nature columns for a small local paper—is characterized by clichés and pedantry. He also senses that marriage has been disappointing for Nancy (133) and that he has failed Viola (125), yet he is a good man who takes nothing for granted. He had "resolved that he would try always to be kind. It was the best he could do. It was all that he could do. And it might be love, after all" (282). For Atkinson, this may well be the substance of Teddy's heroism: "For me, Teddy's heroism is that he survived and he carried on" (NPR 2015). Of course, there is much of Teddy's life that we don't hear about, especially the years after Nancy's death. What we do get is his sense of the past to that point, so how the war altered the lives of participants becomes most apparent. Nancy gave up a promising career in mathematics for the war—she excelled at Bletchley Park, where British intelligence worked to break German codes (78, 290)—and then for Teddy and Viola (291). For Teddy, the war erased the person he was and made him something else: "The truth was there was nothing else he wanted to do, could do. Flying on bombing raids had *become* him. Who he was" (262). For Teddy, everything is an afterward he must dutifully endure: "He had been reconciled to death during the war and then suddenly the war was over and there was a next day and a next day and a next day. Part of him never adjusted to having a future" (96). And as an aging man, he circles back in his memories to the war, to the raids on which he lost friends (Turino, Hamburg, Nuremburg), and to the loss of his wife.

Memory, however, is always memory of something and for something. That is, what is remembered and how it is remembered serves a purpose in the present. This is true for individuals and for collectivities. Teddy and Viola remember things very differently for different reasons (he is often surprised by comments Viola makes in interviews [126, 322]), and Nancy becomes frustrated by Teddy's "making memories" (299) after he learns of her prognosis, but she is equally desirous that Viola know things about her such as the bluebell being her favorite flower (297), for as memories fade and individuals die, objects are left to embody their silent stories. Collective memory, in this case the British memory of the war and particular aspects of it such as the Blitz or the bombing campaign, have been probed by a number of novelists, historians, film makers, and others over the last few decades as once-classified material comes into the public domain and as some of the war's enduring myths are exposed by skeptical audiences. Of course, one cannot ignore the twin facts that those who survived the war are dying while the power and prestige of the victorious nations have significantly waned. The contemporary reevaluation of historical events that seeped into collective memory through aggressive wartime and then Cold War propaganda alters our understanding of those events by providing a corrective to those simpler accounts.

Hence, many more recent treatments look, as Atkinson's novels do, to aspects of the war that were either overlooked or sanitized to fit a particular heroic narrative. Novels such as *Life After Life,* Sarah Waters's *The Night Watch,* or Helen Humphrey's *Coventry* look at the Blitz, while McEwan's *Atonement* looks at the disaster of Dunkirk. *A God in Ruins* deals with the bombing campaign and notes in several places that it has become a controversial aspect of the Allied war effort because of doubts about both its efficacy and, more importantly, its morality.[12] Tellingly, a memorial to the bombing campaign to honor those who fought and perished in it was dedicated in Green Park, London, only in June of 2012. Atkinson coordinates Teddy's death with the dedication of the Green Park Memorial (Bertie sees some of the dignitaries' cars pass her and notices the fly over [363], but she watches the actual dedication later on the news), but Atkinson does not shy away from the campaign's horrors which Teddy fully recognizes (212).

Life After Life and *A God in Ruins* participate in this reevaluation of the war experience in a necessarily limited fashion: as she confides in the "Author's Note" to *A God in Ruins,*

> When I first decided that I wanted to write a novel set during the Second World War, I rather grandiosely believed that I could somehow cover the whole conflict in less than half the length of *War and Peace.* When I realized this was too daunting a challenge—for both reader and writer—I chose the two aspects of the war that interested me most and which I thought provided the richest material—the London Blitz and the strategic bombing campaign against Germany. (385)

In fact, she does go slightly outside these two frames, especially in the account in *Life After Life* of Ursula's life in Germany toward the end of the war. The advantage that fiction has over more comprehensive historical accounts is that it can present a sense of how events were experienced—it is not the truth, but it does convey something of what would otherwise be lost as time passes, and so fiction, novels, become part of a society's collective memory store; as Atkinson said, referring to the reticence of those who experienced the war, "I admire that reticence but it has robbed us today of much understanding of what their experiences [were]. Now, as that generation approaches its end those experiences are slipping even further from view. Fiction is a (rather poor) attempt at facsimile. The imagination is an act of rescue but by necessity it must render fact through its own lens" ("Baileys Women's Prize," n.d.). In *A God in Ruins,* memory of the war is registered privately in Teddy's thoughts, politically in war monuments (such as at Runnymede or Green Park[13]) and other markers and in the public celebration of tradition such as the Queen's jubilee. Individual objects found and passed on—emerald earrings, for instance, or, more significantly, the silver hare passed from Ursula to Teddy to Sunny, who will give it to Viola "For luck. For protection" (372)—embody personal and familial memories and, in the case of the earrings, point to a larger history, but personal and collective memory accedes to historical memory as time passes, and *A God in Ruins* exists on the cusp of this transition. Teddy remembers the war, but he has also read histories of the war (211, 279); at the same time, cultural attitudes about the bombing campaigns in Europe have shifted.

The question of what and how events, especially those of national significance, are remembered often poses challenges. Personal memories, as Marita Sturken suggests, can come into conflict with cultural memories and then with memory inscribed in historical discourse (5). "Survivors stand at the juncture of cultural memory and history" (1997, 12). These three forms of remembering bleed into each other as personal memories can become cultural artifacts and then the material of historical discourse.[14] Teddy is, of course, a survivor of Bomber Command, but much of his experience, his memory of the war, is unexpressed and deliberately concealed. Similarly, Bomber Command's role in the war was not acknowledged in Churchill's victory speech when he recognized those units that contributed to the Allied victory in Europe. The Green Park memorial was built with private funds, often from veterans. In writing her novel Atkinson contributes to the cultural remembering of something that there has been some reluctance to think about, and consequently personal stories are shared carefully, if at all. (Viola's condemnation is certainly not isolated.[15]) The presence of a memorial, however, as Sturken points out, has the paradoxical effect of reviving a language of heroism, fraternity, and patriotic sacrifice that can justify, even excuse a dubious martial tactic as unpleasant moral issues and difficult opinions are easily obscured. Forgetting is, then, a part of remembering. But personal stories will get lost if they are not made a part of a community's remembrance. Objects and mementos that can seemingly preserve memory lose that power if they are detached from narrative and left to be found among one's things by survivors. Teddy's goldfish patch pops into his memory a few times, including on the occasion when he won a goldfish for Viola at a farm fair (167), and then he used it to help console Viola when the fish died (175); the patch is found among his medals by Sunny, who takes them in a moment of teenage anger because he considers himself deprived of the opportunity for heroism (154). Part of what happens is that the war experience defies its representation for any who did not share in its horrors. Teddy cannot write about it in a novel (90), and he can never explain why, for instance, he chopped a flowering lilac on the first of April: "then she [Nancy] saw the look in his eyes and realized it was something from the war—the great fall from grace—and he was unlikely to explain it" (291).[16] He tells Bertie the stain on a photograph of Nancy, the dog Lucky, and himself, is tea (262), although we later learn it is Keith's blood (281). With Teddy's passing, however, survivors will see the photo, assuming it survives, as stained with tea, so another part of Keith will disappear from view and from memory. The war's trauma, it seems, cannot be shared beyond the community of veterans. And even then, when Teddy attends a reunion dinner, he finds himself unable to advance a discussion of the bombing campaign's merits. Meeting his Canadian navigator, Donald "Mac" McLintock, Teddy finds his doubts about the campaign, inspired by his reading, met with derision: "'Can't believe you've joined the hand-wringers, Ted.' . . . 'They started it, Ted,' Mac said. . . . It was the backstop to every argument. They started it. They sowed the wind. They asked for it. The clichés thrown up by war" (211).[17] There is a layering of understanding that Atkinson presents: civilians, combatants, and historians look at events from different places. When Keith and Teddy have tea at Fox Corner, one of Sylvie's guests, a local councilor, refers to the bombing of Hamburg as a "good show. . . . a great success for the RAF" (270). Teddy and Keith's experience of the raid is quite different, told in anachronous analepses while the lunch is described, for them the burning city was "a medieval apocalypse. . . . The smoke and the soot of the fire had risen up to meet them thousands of feet in the air. And the something else, something that Teddy would never forget, something he could never talk about—the smell of burning flesh rising from the pyre" (279–80). Teddy leaves his mother's luncheon to escape the banality. Later, histories will teach him about the raid: "he learned that it had been a 'firestorm.' He had not heard that word, not during the war" (279).[18] Teddy's own judgment about the value of the bombing campaign is confused, but he knows "Hamburg wasn't a turning point, it was a staging post. In the end it led to Tokyo, it led to Hiroshima, and then . . ." (279). With Ursula during the war, he refuses to entertain doubts about "area bombing" (277–78), and even after meeting Mac at the reunion, Teddy knows he would do it all again, although he doesn't say so (212), yet he has learned enough to develop skepticism about the campaign. Nonetheless, he remains faithful to the memories of his friends on his aircrews, especially Keith. At this level, the war is not about patriotism or heroism but about love and loyalty to one's comrades.

The photograph taken of Teddy, Nancy, and Lucky during a brief leave (261) embodies the problems associated with remembering and with its re-inscription. That is to say, the photo's meaning is altered with time. Initially it captures the couple in a time from which neither expects to emerge. Teddy recalls that there was no sense of an "afterward" during the war (72). Indeed, the war had largely effaced his sense of self (262). Nancy, too, is altered by the war insofar as the Official Secrets Act prohibits her from sharing any of the details of her work. Teddy speculates correctly that, as a talented mathematician, she is helping to break German codes (115), but he is frustrated by the banality of her letters. As well, Nancy had given up Teddy for dead when he was shot down: she had no expectation of a future with him. Indeed, despite the war's life-altering effects, neither can reveal or communicate how they were affected: "their relationship foundered on ignorance" (77). The matter is assumed: Nancy comes to expect Teddy's nightmares (97) and recognizes the intrusion of the war into his thoughts while, for Teddy, Nancy always seems a mystery concealing something: "Show me your workings, Nancy, he thought" (177). The photo, then, as Roland Barthes notes, is marked by death, the consciousness that it reflects an absence, that the moment it depicts is gone, that the body depicted is no longer there in space or substance (1994, 9, 14–15). Teddy kept the picture with him throughout the war and after, when Nancy (and Lucky) are indeed dead. The addition of the blood stain literally marks the image as a memorial to the dead. As with his use of the goldfish patch, Teddy avoids revealing the truth of his war experience and, perhaps intentionally, prevents its co-optation into a story of heroic sacrifice and patriotism, which would, he knows, reduce horror and moral ambiguity to a "bloody good show."

Teddy's photograph has a corresponding one depicting Sunny, Bertie, and Teddy's dog, Tinker, that Sunny finds in the box with Teddy's medals and other things (153–54). Sunny, touched by the memory of Tinker, takes the photo along with the medals because they remind him of his trip with his grandfather to Stonefall, the Commonwealth War Graves Commission cemetery where Keith is buried (144–48). Sunny, a troubled adolescent, is surprised he enjoyed the cemetery and the trip because they both awakened a curiosity about his grandfather's life he had not felt before.

As her comments appended to both *Life After Life* and *A God in Ruins* reveal, Atkinson is an astute reader of her work. She notes image patterns (such as the red ribbon), key words ("constraint," "restraint," "freedom" [*A God in Ruins* 388]), and comments on thematic concerns. We also get some insight into her values as a novelist: "I believe in the rich textural (and textual) interplay of plot, character, narrative, theme and image and all the other ingredients that get thrown in the pot, but I don't believe that necessarily makes me a traditionalist. . . . Imagery is for me of paramount importance" (*A God in Ruins* 387). Atkinson's belief in the interplay of plot, character, narrative, theme, and image stands in contrast to the views of many postmodernist or perhaps metafictional American writers in the 1960s, many of whom she studied. Most notably, John Hawkes declared in an interview that "the true enemies of the novel were plot, character, setting and theme" (1965, 149). That comment is often taken to mean more than Hawkes surely intended, but in its radical expression it reminds us of Virginia Woolf's "Modern Fiction" as well: "if [a writer] could write what he chose, not what he must, . . . there would be no plot, no comedy, no tragedy, no love interest or catastrophe in the accepted style" (Woolf 150). The difference lies in the fact that Woolf's interest is in conveying the experience of life as it is lived, which involves a high degree of subjectivity. Hawkes's view is oriented to the medium—language—and emphasizes its playful possibilities without the obligation of verisimilitude (arguments Archie McCue explained in *Emotionally Weird*). Atkinson's assertion in her note following *A God in Ruins* separates her at this stage of her career from the overt playfulness of her earlier work. As Micir observes, Atkinson's academic devotion to American postmodern fiction has been taken as guidance to her own proclivities in her writing, but in commentary she has doubted, usually with reference to Sterne, the usefulness of the concept (e.g., "Author's Note" 387). It isn't that language play has left her, but the subjects of *Life After Life* and *A God in Ruins* demand textual and narrative respect. Novels, she reminds us, are not history, but Atkinson has taken pains, signaled in the extensive acknowledgments and bibliographies appended to both novels, to represent the experiences of the Blitz and Bomber Command accurately. The playfulness comes in the narrative shifting in *Life After Life*'s case from life to life and in *A God in Ruins*' case from the present moment, to memory, to proleptic details about the future. In the latter novel, too, we see the mixing of discourses that we also found in *Emotionally Weird.* In *A God in Ruins,* parts of an Augustus novel and excerpts from Teddy's "Nature Notes," under the byline Agrestis (92), are presented within the narrative's larger discourse. As well, late in the novel, we learn that Bertie, who works in advertising, carries "a ragbag of loveliness . . . around . . . to protect herself from the evil materialist universe" (358). The "ragbag" is actually a small anthology of verse, recalling *The Rattlebag* (1982), which was edited by Ted Hughes and Seamus Heaney, so lines from English poetry filter into the book's latter part through Bertie's consciousness and her reading. When Teddy is dying, bits of the verse she reads him underscore what is already a moving sequence (371) while, slightly earlier, lines of poetry are juxtaposed to the vacuous jargon of advertising and business when Bertie attends a meeting (358).

The question of fiction's obligation to truth is raised early in *A God in Ruins* —even before the narrative opens, in fact, for one of three epigraphs is credited to Sylvie Beresford Todd: "The purpose of Art is to *convey* the truth of a thing, not to *be* the truth itself." The remark comes from a family discussion in the book's second segment ("1925 Alouette"), and the question of art's purpose is raised in a few places in the novel. What is striking about the epigraphs is that the other two are from Ralph Waldo Emerson's *Nature* (the source of the book's title) and Robert Baden-Powell's *Scouting for Boys,* so a fictional character is positioned between actual people. (Atkinson does the same thing in *Life After Life,* with a remark by Edward Beresford Todd following quotations from Nietzsche and Plato.) In the case of Teddy's experience as a pilot, it is the feeling that fiction can express that is important, although historical details may be incorrect or adapted.[19]

Some of what challenges our interpretations as we read is due to the narrating voice, which is often witty, ironical, and occasionally judgmental. Kindness is one of Teddy's self-defining qualities (282), but Viola is presented unsympathetically through most of the book. We are baldly told that she is seldom honest with herself (131), and earlier one of her thoughts is followed with the comment "skillfully converting selfishness to altruism" (65); a bit later she imagines "the Ancient Mariner was lucky—his albatross was already dead before it was hung round his neck"(322). One could multiply the examples. Viola is one of Atkinson's "bad mothers"—by Viola's own admission, which Bertie agrees with (239, 329), as does the narrator: "She had been waiting for her father to die so her life could begin, but as we could all have told her it doesn't work like that" (369). Nonetheless, Viola is somewhat redeemed late in the novel when she abruptly decides after ten years of not seeing him to visit Sunny in Bali, and eventually, after hearing of Teddy's death, she tells Sunny about a dream she had on the plane to Singapore:

> "And then you turned to me and you were smiling and you said, 'We did it, Mum! Everyone got on the train.'"
>
> "I don't think it was about the train."
>
> "No," Viola agreed. "It was how I felt you when you spoke to me."
>
> "Which was?"
>
> "Overwhelmed by love. For you."
>
> Oh, Viola. At last. (370)

In that last comment, the narrator's relief appears almost palpable, and Viola becomes more than a caricature.

Teddy's essential goodness does not exempt him from error or guilt, as his suspicions about Nancy's fidelity make clear. Her sense of her life with Teddy is also part of the narrative focus and provides some keenly felt contrast between parallel moments that are narrated separately but converge in Nancy's statement, "No, Teddy. You don't know. You don't know anything" (182, 296). Nancy, we have already learned, has a brain tumor and has kept this diagnosis from Teddy until he confronts her (182). He has assumed she has been having an affair but her sisters—Gertie, Bea, Millie, and even Ursula—all know she has been seeing doctors and having tests to determine the cause of debilitating headaches, and they have urged her to tell Teddy what is happening (295). As readers, we do not share Teddy's suspicions because the narrator has often referred to Nancy's headaches, her premature death, and the consequences for Viola, but Teddy does not have that knowledge. Consequently, his suspicions can be frustrating for readers and point to his limitations, however understandable his error. Guilt, too, plagues him: he feels he has failed Viola as a parent (125) and worries that he did not offer Nancy the life she wanted (133). And then there are the troublesome moral questions that his war experience raises. On a personal level, he recalls a brief secret affair he had during the war with the beautiful and rich, but shallow, Julia, who enjoyed his attentions for a week before ending their mostly physical relationship (266–69). More generally, Viola levels the moral arguments about the bombing against her father, but for Teddy they are divorced from the intensely personal experience of the war and those who fought it, particularly lost friends and especially Vic and Keith.

Teddy seldom expresses his experiences in the war to others, and this aspect of the trauma war inflicts is found in many places in *Life After Life* and *A God in Ruins.* Hugh, Izzie, Ursula, Teddy, and Jimmy, Ursula and Teddy's younger brother, are all reticent about the war. Jimmy, we glean from Teddy's thoughts, landed on D-day at Sword Beach and his unit had liberated Bergen-Belsen. He "and Teddy had never spoken about that, had barely spoken about the war. [Teddy] wished they had" (138; Bertie also thinks about Jimmy's life [360]). Sometimes, though, an unspoken understanding exists among those who were involved in the fighting. For instance, Sylvie's dismissive comment about Izzie's war is undercut by the narrator's filling in some relevant background material during a discussion of cowardice, or "'LMF,' . . . Lack of Moral Fibre. Waverers. When the nerves get the better of men in the services, but they call it cowardice" (108):

> "I saw a lot of that in the trenches," Izzie said.
>
> "You weren't *in* the *trenches,*" Sylvie said. . . . Only Hugh, surprisingly, had had some tolerance for 'Izzie's war,' as he referred to it. He had come across her once, during the horror of the Somme, at an advanced dressing station. . . . "Oh, look at you, you're alive, how wonderful! I won't kiss you, I'm awfully filthy, I'm afraid." She had tears in her eyes and at that moment Hugh forgave his sister for many future, and as yet unmade, mistakes.
>
> . . .
>
> "The *men* were in the trenches," Sylvie persisted, "not a few genteel lady volunteers."
>
> "The First Aid and Nursing Yeomanry were not genteel ladies," Izzie said, unruffled. "We got our hands very dirty. And it's a terrible thing to label a man a coward," she added quietly. (109)

Izzie "never told anyone at home" (26) about the Croix de Guerre she was awarded, so its discovery after her death coupled with the bequest of her estate to her granddaughter, "a woman in Germany" (151), stand as twin mysteries for her surviving relatives. Similarly, Hugh does not speak of the first war; Nancy is restrained by the Official Secrets Act; and Teddy, while desirous to write a novel, cannot conceive of "something so shattering" being rendered into fiction (90). Ursula, too, says little of the Blitz and conceals statistics about casualties in Bomber Command from Teddy (she hears the figures in *Life After Life,* 404, 410, 414). For those who participated in either war, the experience is life altering, even in small ways: Teddy, for instance, refuses to purchase German-made products long after the war.[20]

Teddy's resistance to writing about the war is qualified by the narrator—Teddy cannot imagine "that something so shattering in its reality could be rendered so quickly into fiction" (90). His conversation with Nancy about his writing occurs in the chapter "1947 The Unforgiving Winter," so the "so quickly" has its justification. Atkinson's two novels, however, like those of her contemporaries such as Ian McEwan, Sarah Waters, and others, of course, no longer face the prohibition Teddy felt. Again, the point is to convey the truth of the thing as it was felt to be the truth. Novels are not history, whether political, cultural, martial, or even social. The felt life, though, can be conveyed in art. Teddy's war is never wholly related to us. His experiences emerge in the discourse in fragmentary memories so that by the time we do get a more complete accounting, as we do of the Nuremburg raid, for instance, or the meaning behind the Goldfish Club (his damaged plane ditched in the water returning from a mission), we, like Teddy, already have bits of information in our memory that we can recall. From another perspective, we are presented with glimpses of the future of which the characters in the immediate narrative frame are unaware. The matter is doubly reinforced if we are familiar with the Todds from *Life After Life*. Consequently, an ironic perspective is again brought to the reader and, while it mitigates narrative suspense, it also allows us to see more than the present moment; time again is a palimpsest.

The final twist in *A God in Ruins* is unsettling in that it detaches readers from what we had been encouraged to care about. Readers of *Life After Life* were taught by the book to understand such abrupt narrative ruptures. In its companion novel, we have not been acculturated to drastic changes in the characters' fates. Still, Viola's presence as a novelist in *A God in Ruins* does give us the mirror in the text that implicitly reminds us that we are reading a novel. She often notes images (309), phrases (132), and possible titles (322) she might use, and, of course, she feels that writing a war novel will benefit her critical reputation. Yet Viola is so vile through most of the book that we probably do not credit these passages about her with the kind of self-reflexive importance that would be a key to the narrative's ending, which, of course, is not really an ending at all, as we circle back from Ursula's reading of a chapter in an Augustus story, which ends on page 384, to the same moment on page 40. But even without that, the possibility that Teddy might be reincarnated in the skylark Ursula and Nancy see offers the possibility of another vision and so mitigates our uneasiness.

Transcription

Lighter in tone than the previous two novels, *Transcription* returns to the Second World War but characteristically moves in three different time periods—briefly in 1981, then alternates events of 1950 with those of 1940. Those sections have different plots but some overlapping characters, as Juliet Armstrong finds that events from her wartime work are echoing in the postwar world. The last fifty pages or so resolve lingering questions in briefer sections, again identified as "1940" and "1950," and provide an entirely unexpected plot twist.

A brief description of the narrative will help to contextualize my further comments. With the onset of the war, Juliet Armstrong had hoped to enlist in one of the women's armed services (31) but instead found herself mysteriously selected for an interview with Miles Merton and then work in the British intelligence service MI5, along with several other young women, one of whom is Clarissa, who becomes a close friend. (Clarissa is the fourth daughter of a duke, and, with Atkinson's characteristic allusiveness, Juliet—aware of Samuel Richardson's eighteenth-century books—asks if Clarissa has a sister named Pamela, which she does [38]). Anticipating life as a spy, Juliet finds herself instead a small piece in a huge bureaucracy and is confined to the clerical work of typing and filing ("It would be menials who would win this war, she thought, not girls in pearls" [40]; or, as Ursula puts it in *Life After Life,* "Without the cog there is no machine" [406]) until she is chosen seemingly at random by Peregrine Gibbons (called Perry) to join a special surveillance operation tracking the activities of fifth columnists, British citizens who sought to assist Germany's war against Britain. Again, Juliet's work is largely clerical, although the sexism of the period also has her doing errands such as preparing tea, dusting, emptying ashtrays, and generally cleaning up messes. Juliet also ends up taking care of a dog named Lily, a duty she shares with her coworker Cyril, an audio technician. (The dog belongs to a Hungarian woman, Nelly Varga, who is acting as a double agent. Her devotion to the animal held by British intelligence ensures that Varga will return and continue to operate as an agent.[21]) More importantly, Juliet is tasked with transcribing recorded conversations between a British agent, Godfrey Toby (an assumed name), and Nazi sympathizers who believe they are meeting with a Gestapo agent. Juliet's work is tedious and the conversations are often mundane (excerpts of the work are printed in a Courier font), but Juliet is soon asked to pose as a fifth columnist herself to infiltrate the social world of another group of people and to get particularly close to a Mrs. Scaife. This being a book about intelligence operations in the early days of the war, however, we soon discover that MI5 is still learning its job. Its identifying code for agents—"Can I tempt you?," to be answered with, "That's very kind of you. I think I will" (82)—proves woefully inadequate because the question is so common. Indeed, Juliet's first use of it becomes farcical when her response invites unwanted attentions from a man who thinks she is a prostitute. The result is a kind of tug-of-war, with Juliet being pulled between the gentleman and the woman, Mrs. Ambrose, whom Juliet was supposed to meet (83–84). There is a kind of improvisational aspect to MI5, especially when some unanticipated deaths occur, but by 1950 the service's effectiveness is much improved. Still, readers are aware of the technological gulf that exists between the war and, by implication, the present: the recording equipment at the Dolphin Square apartment takes up a small room (42) and reports are typed in triplicate with carbon paper, but there is microfilm, a camera in a cigarette lighter, a cane concealing a rapier, and, for Godfrey's Nazi sympathizers, invisible ink (which pleases them). But in the "looking-glass" (42) world of espionage, nothing can be taken at face value, and Juliet and readers discover how difficult it is to discern what is trustworthy. Perry warns Juliet that Merton cannot be trusted (53), but "the mark of a good agent is when you have no idea which side they're on" (116, 223).

The "1950" sections of the novel center on Juliet's work at the BBC, which she and the discourse link to MI5 (both are large, labyrinthine corporations, and several former employees of the intelligence service now work at the latter): "Sometimes you had to wonder if MI5 was using the BBC for its own purposes. Or, indeed, if it was the other way round" (214). A chance encounter in the street with Godfrey Toby, who refuses to recognize her (14–15), and anonymous threatening notes soon push Juliet to investigate a possible relationship between the two because she erroneously suspects the notes might be connected to Godfrey's wartime fifth columnists. At the same time, we learn that Juliet occasionally provides a "safe house" for individuals whom MI5 needs to secret for brief periods. So, while she left the service after the war, she really hasn't left—indeed, she can't—and in a book where nothing can be taken at face value but also where connections abound, we and she are never sure whether something occurs by chance, is deliberate, or is part of a much larger plan. Echoing the philosophical and literary enthusiasm of her period, Juliet (and Atkinson, of course) often thinks of Jean-Paul Sartre and particularly his play *Huis Clos* (1944, usually translated as *No Exit*) (224, 230, 311, 317). The references foreground the existential dilemma of choice that resonates so strongly in the novel (of sides, of action, of political allegiance).

As is the case with the earlier books, *Transcription* is allusive and witty. There is an attention to language in Juliet's thoughts that foregrounds language itself in the discourse. She is well aware of Perry's, others', and her own tortured metaphors ("She sighed and chastised herself for a sub-standard metaphor" [188]), and Juliet often thinks of rhymes for names and words she hears: for example, "It was Cyril (rhymes with squirrel . . .)" (42) or "I practice to deceive, she thought. Rhymes with Eve" (148). Like other Atkinson protagonists, she examines idioms and clichés with an amusing literal mindedness: the phrase "you've got a good eye" (or "ear," and other variants, such as "keep an eye out for . . ." [100]) is noted as a joke ("I have two") (33, 52). Similarly, the phrase "Minister without portfolio" is said to evoke the idea of a man who has left his portfolio on the Tube (54), while "cat got your tongue" she finds puzzlingly grotesque (135). Even punctuation is noted: "'This is a Jew's War' . . . (Which one, Juliet wondered, looking at the apostrophe [on a poster].)" (115). Allusions to and echoes of a vast range of texts (even some of Atkinson's own[22]) are also woven throughout; indeed, one of the things Juliet notices about two of her possible romantic partners is the degree to which they are acquainted with Shakespeare's work (Perry, no [70]; Harry, a tall detective, yes [303]). Atkinson's wit is also apparent;

for instance, Fräulein Rosenfeld, at another character's funeral, "was dressed in an odd assortment of black garments, as if she had simply raided her wardrobe for everything in that colour and then piled it all on. She looked like a large rather distressed bat" (256). (Rosenfeld is a German refugee also employed at the BBC in 1950. When she is described earlier, we read, "The burden of Europe was on her dowager's hump. It weighed heavily" [208]—a piece of description that recalls something Angela Carter said about her character Mignon in *Nights at the Circus* [in Haffenden 1985, 87][23].) Ubiquitous metaphors associated with theater throughout the text aptly suit the world of cover stories and false identities that characterize espionage while also raising self-reflexive questions about the relationship of fiction with truth, and so in some measure the book is about genre, the narration of history, and fiction itself.

Reviews of *Transcription* tended to see it as another example of Atkinson delving into genre fiction and, in this case, the spy novel, but she resists that, claiming, as she similarly did in discussions of *Case Histories* as a crime novel, that *Transcription* is not a spy novel but a novel that happens to have spies in it (Toronto appearance). Juliet is an unlikely recruit for MI5, although she was accomplished in school and in her secretarial college. (We learn very late in the book that she had been recommended to Merton by her headmistress at school [314].) She certainly is not the university type that we see recruited into the intelligence service in other novels, as was Serena Frome in Ian McEwan's *Sweet Tooth,* for example, or even Nancy in *A God in Ruins.* Juliet's mother's illness and death when Juliet was seventeen curtailed her academic career (her father is described only as a merchant seaman who drowned before her birth), and most of her interview with Miles Merton consists of her lies, which she learns later he recognized (36–37, 308). She is, then, young and on her own, self-sufficient but also naive, especially about sexual matters. Having absorbed most of her knowledge of romantic relationships from her mother's romance novels (references are made in several places to these texts [41, 44, 77, 101]), Juliet is incredibly blind to Perry's homosexuality, even when it is openly referred to by those around her and even when she sees evidence of it (151). But like many of Atkinson's young women, Juliet is witty and precociously resourceful, even "plucky" (136). Transcribing recorded conversations offers little opportunity for creativity, but one of the things Juliet does is fill in gaps when the recorded conversations are garbled or inaudible: "Quite a bit of guesswork. Sometimes she wondered if she just wasn't making things up, filling in the gaps to make sense of it" (60). She speculates that she might very well be able to make the whole thing up, and, after Dolly's and her dog's deaths, she finds ways to keep them in the records. Similarly, she often imagines herself as participating in some sort of stage show (e.g., 156, 169) because of the many roles she has to play, which marks her as another of Atkinson's fiction-creating characters.

While the novel does revisit the war, *Transcription* is sometimes self-consciously farcical, as events in the tea room show, so the overall feeling is something closer to Graham Greene's *Our Man in Havana* (1958) than John le Carré's *The Spy Who Came in From the Cold* (1963). The aspect of the war dealt with here tended to slip from view after the fall of France, the Battle of Britain, and the Blitz. Indeed, as the war goes on, Juliet, Cyril, and Godfrey begin to feel as if they have been forgotten (301). Fifth columnists were, of course, a concern during the war, and especially so in the period known as the Phoney War (September 1939 to May 1940), when there was more anticipation of what was to come than actual fighting. Atkinson's "Author's Note" reveals that, while doing research for *A God in Ruins,* she came across transcripts of interviews "Jack King" had with Nazi sympathizers. "Jack King" was, in fact, a man named Eric Roberts who worked as a clerk at Westminster Bank but who was also with MI5. As she read through the typescripts, she realized the typist would undoubtedly be a girl and that such anonymous figures were employed throughout the government as part of the war effort. The material Juliet transcribes in the novel is based on released transcripts but is fiction and betrays a kind of pathetic egotism and a naive and foolish understanding of Nazi policies in those who consider themselves the vanguard of a remade country once Germany conquers. While a rapid overview of Juliet's, her coworkers', and friends' war years reminds us of the war's horrors, Atkinson cannot help but foreshadow them in comments from Trude, one of the Nazi sympathizers Godfrey regularly meets, who longs for Germany to rain bombs on London and who suggests that Jews be burned (110). Atkinson's foreshadowing is also seen, more particularly, in Perry's brief etymological lesson at Verulamium: "'A very well-preserved mosaic floor. It covers the hypocaust. *Hypocaustrum* from the Ancient Greek—*hypo* meaning "beneath" and *caust* "burnt." Which word do you think we get from that?'" (146, echoed 228).[24]

Godfrey and the narrative itself, acknowledging the banality of evil, stress that these would-be Nazis are "ordinary people" with their own preoccupations and motives, and many were associated with various right-wing groups in Britain prior to the war, the British Union of Fascists being one of the more prominent, though it is the more Establishment-oriented Right Club that features in the novel. Still, the fifth columnists are far from the caricatures of Nazi spies that a film such as *Notorious* might provide. Juliet finds Mrs. Scaife motherly and imagines "if it weren't for her rabid anti-Semitism or her worship of Hitler, they might have got on" (87). Juliet also wonders if she would believe what Mrs. Scaife and her companions believe, if she'd been brought up in their world (87). The thought raises questions about how our beliefs are formed, but it is worth noting that, of her two children, Mrs. Scaife's son is "rather left-leaning" (87) and part of the RAF (as a Lancaster bomber captain, he was lost over Berlin

[263]). Atkinson presents Juliet's first meeting with Mrs. Scaife as marked by typical class biases and the ordinariness of "Englishwomen doing what Englishwomen did best whenever they were in the world—taking tea and having cosy chats" (85). Mrs. Scaife's anti-Semitism is fueled by one of history's most notorious frauds, *The Protocols of the Elders of Zion,* a copy of which she gives to Juliet who has already been prepared with it by Perry (86). Members of the Right Club and Mrs. Scaife's circle sing their own version of "Land of Hope and Glory" whenever they are present during the anthem's playing, which makes Juliet very uncomfortable (118). But anti-Semitic views are often observed to be casually and ubiquitously expressed in many quarters of British society and not just by fascists: "A butcher in the East End had recently displayed a sign that said 'If you eat pork you're welcome here,' an anti-Semitic message that proved too subtle for most of his customers" (90). Juliet thinks that "it must be awfully handy to have a scapegoat for the world's ills. (*Women and Jews tend to be first in line, unfortunately.*)" (88, italics in original).

The separation that italics provide points to two levels of narration or, perhaps, two narrating voices, one of which sometimes mirrors Juliet's thoughts while another often provides disembodied comment on the main narrative line. This separation mirrors the split in Juliet, who, in meetings with Mrs. Scaife, assumes the identity of Iris Carter-Jenkins, a role Perry and MI5 have calculated to appeal to Mrs. Scaife. But the italicized comments can provide some extratextual reflection. Hitler had at one time been regarded as "a harmless clown," although in a parenthetical addition, "('The clowns are the dangerous ones,' Perry said.)" (86); and slightly later, another of Perry's remarks is recalled, "('Do not equate nationalism with patriotism,' Perry warned Juliet. 'Nationalism is the first step on the road to Fascism.')" (87). For readers, Juliet's parenthetically presented reflections gloss the conversation Iris is having with Mrs. Scaife and Mrs. Ambrose, another of Perry's operatives, so we again get two lines of interpretation presented to us.

Role-playing is a ubiquitous practice within MI5. Godfrey Toby, Mrs. Ambrose, and Juliet all have assumed identities. Godfrey Toby and Mrs. Ambrose are their MI5 names, which are what they are known by throughout the novel. Early on Godfrey is described as "rather good at evasion" (23) and "'The Great Enigma' . . . 'a master of obfuscation,'" according to Hartley, one of Juliet's acquaintances within MI5 (47). Perry's name is not altered, but his double life is quickly apparent to readers and to most of the other characters, excepting Juliet: he is a closeted gay man living in a straight world who, through social appearances, dinners, excursions, and ultimately engagement, uses Juliet to conceal his true self. Several remarks and puns emphasize Perry's plight—he is described as a "queer fish" early on (44) and later, when he has gone missing just before his arrest, we are told he's "closeted somewhere" (275). Juliet's naiveté about such matters offers opportunities for humor in the text when, for example, she expects seduction on a trip to look at otters. Humor aside, Perry's situation is developed sympathetically. While he seems to feel some self-loathing (115), he is presented as a first-rate agent and kind to Juliet. The fact of his homosexuality is well known among people in the agency—"Oh, sweetie, everyone knows" (299)—but hardly a matter of concern to his coworkers except that he got caught; consequently, he was consigned to an "outer circle of hell" in the Ministry of Information (300), but, then, maybe he never left the service (213). In the looking-glass world of espionage (well suited to Atkinson's passion for Lewis Carroll's novels, which are among the many allusions here [e.g., 42, 243]), nothing can be taken at face value, including Juliet's statements.

As her first interview with Merton establishes, Juliet is "good at lying" (287), and the pattern continues to be revealed in small things—when Perry suggests a brief test for Juliet in the Russian tea room near where she lives, he asks, "'Do you know it?' No, she thought. 'Yes,' she said" (80)[25]—and in large when she assumes the identity of Iris Carter-Jenkins to negotiate her relations with Mrs. Scaife and her social set, many of whom are "18b widows," that is, women whose husbands have been interned under Regulation 18b (a defense regulation that allowed the internment of suspected Nazi sympathizers). She also assumes the identity of "Madge Wilson" when she identifies the body of Beatrice Dodds, Mrs. Scaife's murdered maid, as a sister, "Ivy Wilson." Later, after the war, Juliet, "adding another role to her repertoire" (262), allows Mrs. Scaife's daughter Minnie to think that Juliet is "Nightingale," the housemaid who replaced Dodds. At one point, Juliet reflects,

> I have been too many people. . . . The spy Iris Carter-Jenkins a perky, plucky sort of girl. The "beloved sister" Madge Wilson, who had falsely identified poor Beatrice. . . . There had been other identities too, although she never owned up to them in public. And then there was Juliet Armstrong, of course, who some days seemed like the most fictitious of them all, despite being the "real" Juliet. But then what constituted real? Wasn't everything, even this life itself, just a game of deception? (258–59)

Later these comments will have an added resonance when the final pieces of Juliet's spy work are revealed, but for now the text raises obvious questions about identity, the prospect of a malleable self, and reality as a facade: Hartley remarks, "We all have a facade" (235), and Juliet, reminding us of Isobel Fairfax in *Human Croquet,* has a "long-held belief that appearances were invariably deceptive" (188). Everything, then, might very well be a front (179). Later, in reports and transcriptions after Dolly's death, "Fiction and fact become one" (300) because Dolly is written into those documents.

Equally pertinent, the narrator does not always tell us what Juliet is doing. For example, in the book's latter half, after visiting a wool shop where her old wartime acquaintance Mrs. Ambrose is supposedly working, we discover that Juliet has taken "a small sock needle" (240) from its "glass coffin"—the display case that, in a characteristic allusion, reminds Juliet of "Snow White's coffin" (238).[26] While we did read about Juliet's conversation in the shop with the salesclerk (a woman Juliet suspects of working for the service) and her purchase of some wool, the detail of a theft is only mentioned a page or two later. Similarly, she pockets the diamond earrings loaned to her so she could fit in at Mrs. Scaife's party, but we do not read of her doing this until much later. (Juliet was about to return them to a jeweler but, coincidentally, met Mrs. Scaife in the same shop on the day after the party. Afraid Mrs. Scaife will recognize the earrings, Juliet lies about her reason for being there, but we also suspect Mrs. Scaife is also lying to Juliet when she says she's having some pieces reset [130]; in fact, she is heavily indebted [133]).

These delayed revelations of Juliet's actions that go unreported should put us on our guard, for the implication is that things of consequence are left unsaid—a point particularly pertinent when Juliet hosts "the Flamingo," the Czech scientist who has defected to the West. Of course, delaying the answers to enigmas posed earlier in narrative is a standard way to develop suspense, especially in thrillers where narrative suspense compels an eager reader to continue. In *Transcription,* the end of the first "1940" section (173) and the end of the second "1950" section (270) provide easy narrative suspense, but we are often teased with details, phrases in Juliet's memory, for instance, that only find their context much later. Similarly, information is often offered piecemeal and then more fully later on. One thinks, for example, of the bomb that destroyed the Café de Paris ("Someone she had once been close to had died" [231]; later we learn it was Clarissa [301]), or of the cryptic hints about Dodds' grave (259) that are explained later (288). And Perry's instructions in tradecraft often echo in Juliet's thoughts and so in the text as implied advice to readers. Again, this kind of narrative echoing is not unusual, but it does allow us to see shifting attitudes and meanings when phrases appear in new contexts.

In her note to *Life After Life,* Atkinson wrote that she considered the book in part to be about "being English" (483). In *Transcription,* the phrase "this England" echoes in all three narrative time frames, and, indeed, it can be said to open and close the novel when Juliet, dying on the pavement after being struck by a vehicle, murmurs, "This England" (4, 327). On her excursion with Perry to look at otters, he reflectively asks, "This England . . . Is it worth fighting for, do you think?" (67). Hearing the phrase, Juliet immediately thinks of Shakespeare's *Richard II* and John of Gaunt's speech in act 2, scene 1—an association many readers may also make[27]—but Perry appears not to know Shakespeare, so his question is narrower but nonetheless pertinent, given the wartime context. Juliet later recalls this exchange when working at the BBC as she ponders her own sense of what the country is: "They [those in the Schools division working on the show *Past Lives* intended for children's education] were reinventing England, or perhaps inventing it. A memory rose up . . . Perry Gibbons turning to her and saying, 'This England—is it worth fighting for?' It depended whose side you were on, she supposed" (207).[28] Her ambivalent response here is one moment that may prepare us for the late plot twist, but she is far more definite toward the book's end, when she leaves the country: "Juliet was glad not to be leaving from Dover. To see those white cliffs receding would have been too sentimental, too much of a metaphor for something she no longer entirely understood. This England, is it worth fighting for? Yes, she thought. What other answer was there?" (322). Juliet remains, it seems, an idealist.

As rereading reveals, the book often alerts us to how we should read it, but we initially do not see those warnings as necessarily applying at a level beyond the narrative. Perry's parenthetically recalled "*Never take anything at face value*" (64), and just a few pages earlier we read that Juliet "had learned to read between the lines. But wasn't that where the most important things were said?" (57). As Iris, she is to keep her eyes and ears open for who Mrs. Scaife might be seeing and corresponding with. Perry is particularly interested in getting hold of the Red Book, which is a list of members of the Right Club, mostly from the British Establishment. Ultimately, this goal is achieved when Juliet acts as intermediary in a meeting between Mrs. Scaife and Chester Vanderkamp, an American working at the U.S. Embassy who seeks to pass sensitive documents on to Germany. On her signal the room is raided by police, Special Branch, and MI5 agents; Mrs. Scaife and Vanderkamp are arrested.[29] Prior to this, however, Juliet had attempted to secure the Red Book on her own, with the help of Mrs. Scaife's maid, Beatrice Dodds. The effort proves farcical, and Juliet narrowly escapes being discovered by climbing down a Virginia creeper outside Mrs. Scaife's bedroom window when Mrs. Scaife unexpectedly returns home. Unfortunately, in a Hitchcockian moment, Juliet had left her handbag, Juliet's not Iris's, behind in the living room. She is just able to alert Dodds to its presence before dashing upstairs to the bedroom. What happens to it and Dodds afterward is unclear, but Dodds' body is found with the handbag some days later; she had been strangled with a scarf of the sort Mrs. Scaife wears. What had the trappings of bedroom farce gains, as happens in *Our Man in Havana,* a darker tone.

The events leading up to Dolly's death are equally farcical and grimly absurd. Dolly, too, arrived for her meeting with Godfrey early, and her dog, Dibs, burst in on Juliet and Cyril in the neighboring office apartment. A glance at some typescript and Dolly knows what has been happening. Godfrey arrives and, to keep the operation from being exposed, Dolly is killed—shot initially by Juliet to save Godfrey, then by Cyril as Dolly tries to get away, and finally stabbed by Godfrey, who then kills the frantic Dibs. The three then roll the body into a rug and drive with it upright in the front seat of a car to a cemetery where Dolly and Dibs are added to Dodds' coffin, which is to be buried the next day.[30]

Similarly, the anonymous threats Juliet receives in 1950—mysterious notes warning "you will pay for what you did" (186 and elsewhere)—instill a sense of foreboding, which is then undercut by the mad Nelly Varga's attacks on Juliet because she was responsible for Varga's dog, which ran off terrified during the Blitz. (The dog, cared for by Juliet and Cyril at Dolphin Square, may suggest another possible nod to an earlier text. Cyril and Juliet both imagine alternative fates for the poor creature [302–3]. Although it is presumed killed, readers might think of "Lucky," the dog Ursula rescued in *Life After Life.*) Juliet's sense that she is being stalked, however, is later shown to be accurate, but not in the way she expects, for MI5 is also keeping her under surveillance. Nelly Varga, in a scene that recalls Millie's attack in *Started Early, Took My Dog* that allows Courtney and Tracy to escape at a train station, becomes the unwitting agent of Juliet's escape from British authorities and then, with Perry's and Godfrey's help, from the country (though we and she are never sure of the particulars).

"The spectres of the Cambridge spies stalk [the] halls" ("Author's Note" 331) of Atkinson's narrative, but the big surprise for readers is that Juliet has been passing secrets to the Soviets through Merton and so acting as "mole" within MI5. It is the mark of a good agent not to know whose side she is on, and Juliet is shown to be a good agent. Again, reflecting on the book reveals several places where Juliet's attitudes and sympathies for "menials" and her charitable view of communism are expressed: children, she imagines, have a natural instinct toward it (178), and she defends Klaus Fuchs (a German physicist who was arrested in January 1950 for passing atomic secrets to the Soviet Union) in conversation, which provokes Charles Lofthouse, another BBC employee, to ask, "Whose side are you on, Miss Armstrong?" (186).[31] Her thoughts also reveal a desire for world revolution (88) and a smattering of Marxist thinking: "'People are dying for capitalism?' Prendergast asked curiously. 'Well, people have always died having their labour exploited for other people's profit. . . . Yet what does it all mean in the long run? And religion is the worst offender, of course'" (224). Elsewhere, she thinks of dialectics (215), and very early in the novel she ponders the idea of writing a novel, "But wasn't artistic endeavour the final refuge of the uncommitted?" (20), so she rejects the idea. The obvious implication is that she is committed. After she is unmasked, Mr. Fisher, a shadowy British agent whose paths cross with Juliet's, asserts, "you and Merton and his ilk. You're *intellectual* Communists"; Juliet responds, "It's called idealism, I suppose" (314) but, like other one-time Communists, "I don't believe any more" (314).[32] The question of choosing a "side" turns on the issue of loyalty, which in *Transcription* is framed as an issue of belonging. That is, Juliet is often described as someone's "girl." When applied to Juliet, who has shown herself to be a capable and adept agent, these comments unavoidably resonate with the sexism that diminishes women and presumes them to be either the property of or objects of exchange among men. Such language, however, expressing an individual's assumed loyalty, is common in the service and applied to men as well ("Godfrey is Perry's man" [105]). Nonetheless, when applied to Juliet, it is always a little jarring in our contemporary context to read that Juliet is Perry's girl (105, 321) or Alleyne's girl (236) or Fisher's girl (317). Perhaps, though, Alleyne, another British spy, is proven right, "I don't think you're anyone's girl, Miss Armstrong" (105), for late in the book, after Juliet's encounter with Mr. Fisher, "there were no sides but her own" (319).

As with her previous two novels, Atkinson's "Author's Note" follows the narrative and details some of the ways she combined historical facts with fictional invention. As she said of *Life After Life,* she did a lot of research and then tried to forget it (483). Some names of real fifth columnists are casually mentioned in *Transcription* (William Joyce and Anna Wolkoff, for example), and she does note historical antecedents for events and characters she later developed. Similarly, there were intelligence operations like the one orchestrated at Dolphin Square and the one in search of the Red Book, although Atkinson conflates the two operations into the same locale being carried out by some of the same people. The arrest of Klaus Fuchs as a spy is factual, while notable Cambridge spies go unmentioned, at least by name, although their fictional counterparts share some of their histories. That is, there is no specific mention of Guy Burgess, Donald McLean, or Kim Philby, but Oliver Alleyne's uncovering and defection along with two others clearly echoes their fate. (Philby was suspected in the mid-1950s but, unlike Alleyne, who is said to flee in 1954, Philby defected in 1963.) Historically, a fourth spy, Anthony Blunt, is also suggested by Miles Merton's history. (Blunt, like Merton, had risen to knighthood and was an art historian with several titles. Merton has a position at the National Gallery. Blunt was publicly exposed in late 1979 but had confessed to being a Soviet spy in 1964, a fact that remained secret.) It is Merton's prosecution that has brought Juliet back to England after decades abroad because it had been Merton who recruited her to the Soviet cause following her postwar stretch with the BBC in Manchester. And, as is historically the case, Atkinson includes rumors of a "fifth man" who had assisted not only in these defections but in covering up the existence of these Soviet spies. (The identity of a real "fifth man" has not been definitively established, although there are several possibilities.) In the novel, a fifth man is not identified, although Hartley is a possibility, discounted by Juliet, but the suspicion clouds his career, and then we might remember that he had been a member of the Communist Party while at Cambridge (116).[33] Hartley also participates in the passing of Pavel, "the Flamingo," to the "grey men," and, as Juliet reflects at the time, there had been some confusion about passwords when they set out (198, 203). And, for what it is worth, Hartley drinks heavily.

That Atkinson looks to history for inspiration and plot details is not surprising, but separating fact from fiction is pointless. This is a novel, after all, that at some level is also about fiction, and as a novel about espionage, this quality is doubly true. Fictions are the stuff of MI5's operations, and assumed identities abound. It is very possible that everything is a front for something else (179). Everything Juliet encounters in 1950, such as the mother, Philippa Horrocks, with young children in Godfrey Toby's old house, or the wool shop where Mrs. Ambrose's niece works, appear as a calculated deception. Daisy, the receptionist at the BBC where Juliet works, the cab driver who brings Juliet, Hartley, and the Czech Pavel to the Savoy, Ellen Eckersley at the wool shop: Juliet imagines (or recognizes?) them all as part of the intelligence service. But then another of Perry's pieces of advice was to caution against "fall[ing] prey to delusions and neuroses" (129, 240). Significantly, one of the films Juliet sees when posing as Iris is *Gaslight* (119), and she thinks of it ten years later when she again glimpses the cab driver who earlier in the day took her to the Savoy (212). Who can say, then, what is real and true and what is fiction? As with Juliet's transcriptions after Dolly's death, "Fiction and fact became one" (300).

While the book presents the problem in a number of ways, a telling moment comes near the end in the National Gallery when Merton and Juliet are looking at Rembrandt's "The Night Watch," which is, in fact, a copy of an original that had been cropped to fit a particular space. But, as Merton points out, in this case the copy, the fiction, is truer to the original than the actual picture because the copy was made before the original picture had been altered. The imitation, then, more accurately reflects Rembrandt's vision than the real item. It may be a freakish example, but it points to the relationship between fiction and history that Atkinson has explored here and elsewhere in her books. In a sense, the fictional account can be "truer" than a factual account. "History must have its plot" (180); narrative representations of reality shape our understanding of that reality—a fact Juliet worries about in connection with the radio pieces she works on because they are "reinventing England" (207). The novel interprets history to get at truths that may disappear as individuals die. Notably, in *Transcription,* the question of who is on which side fades as time passes. Juliet's return to England is part of a "tidying up of loose ends" (321), not the rounding up of enemy spies. Even her escape from England in 1950 has little to do with sides but everything to do with relationships. It is more than apparent that Perry, Godfrey Toby, and maybe even Hartley have assisted in her escape because they are loyal to Juliet. (Mr. Fisher remarks that Godfrey was quite protective of her [315].) They all worked with her during the war and in demanding circumstances. Whether they remain in the service or not (and that is not certain), they practice what Greene (1973) called "the virtue of disloyalty"; that is, they place the personal above the political and stand against established power—something Greene sees as the duty of the artist.[34]

Atkinson isn't writing history—it is the spy novel that provides her framing for Juliet's story, but this isn't a story about Juliet's life during the war (we know she has a rich social life with Clarissa, a close friend, but little is revealed about it other than that they have many late nights dancing and drinking). Rather, it is a story about her working life, which is espionage. Reflexively, Juliet imagines herself in a John Buchan or Erskine Childers world (129), undertaking a *Girl's Own* adventure (136, 163), but her approach to espionage may remind us more of Reggie's approach to crime in *When Will There Be Good News?* Both Reggie and Juliet are plucky and resourceful, cool under pressure, and smooth liars. The drole tone throughout *Transcription* keeps the genre's darker associations and models at bay, an oblique allusion through the nursery rhyme to Le Carré's *Tinker, Tailor, Soldier, Spy* near the outset notwithstanding (10). Again, more *Our Man in Havana* in its absurdity, *Transcription* undercuts potentially frightening moments—the anonymous threats Juliet receives, for instance, her frequent sensation of being followed—with a revelation that is anticlimactic but still dangerous: Nelly Varga attacks Juliet in the South Kensington Tube station because her dog had died in Juliet's care (267). Similarly, the earnest efforts of the fifth columnists, motivated largely by personal resentments, stand in contrast to the silly suspicions ordinary folk afflicted with "spy fever" are reporting to the authorities (55). However, as in Greene's novel, unexpected fatalities, first Beatrice Dodds and then Dolly, shake Juliet out of her roles to reveal moral and human struggles (163). Dodds, Dolly, and the latter's dog, Dibs, end up in a common grave marked with a name, Ivy Wilson, that belongs to none of them, and so people are erased from history or, as Juliet later notes, "explained away" (234).

In his fine review in *The New Yorker,* Jonathan Dee suggests that within patriarchy women are accustomed to inhabiting different identities and roles, depending on the context of their relations, and so are well suited to spying. Giselle, "our own Mati Hari" (164), is one example of how a woman can exploit her femininity in the service, but Dee finds the scene in the novel when Juliet and her friend Clarissa, also with MI5 but in a department separate from Juliet's, surprise each other at the same gathering of fascist sympathizers supportive of his argument. Intuitively, Dee suggests, they feign ignorance of the other and pretend to be newly met. Such adaptive abilities are useful in the world of espionage, but it may be a step too far to claim them as the property of women, a point Atkinson has supported in commenting on the novel (Toronto appearance).[35] Certainly, the men in the novel are equally flexible in their assumption of identities and roles. Godfrey Toby, surprised by Dolly while talking to Juliet outside the Dolphin Square apartment, quickly identifies her as a neighbor. In the case of "Mr. Fisher," the man with the "astrakhan collar on an overcoat," we never do learn his proper name nor do we ever grasp his position in the service: "'Who *are* you? You don't seem like MI5.' (But if not, then what?) 'Nothing is as simple as it looks, Miss Armstrong. Surely you, of all people, know that. There can be many layers to a thing. Like the spectrum of light. I exist, you might say, in one of the invisible layers. Think of me in the infra-red'" (312). We only know that he is tied to Godfrey somehow and suggests that his job is to spy on the spies, which may mean he is part of MI6 (315). We also discovered earlier that he knows Iris is Juliet: he interrupts her at the party when she was about to photograph materials on a library desk (why he should have prevented her goes unanswered). In the 1950 section of the narrative, he essentially blackmails Juliet into passing misleading intelligence to Merton (if she doesn't, he would expose her treason), and it is implied that the "Flamingo" is, in part, a setup calculated to expose Juliet as a mole clandestinely passing secrets, through Merton, to the Soviets. (Among Perry's early instructions for Juliet was not to trust Merton [53].) With the "Flamingo," a Czech scientist staying in Juliet's flat, Juliet hopes and assumes it is her last job, but as Merton tells her, "One is never free. It's never *finished*" (311). Mr. Fisher's appearance, which offers the more serious answer to Juliet's concerns about being followed, is then an unintended release insofar as Juliet, after her last job, thinks she can escape. But in true spy thriller fashion, her careful planning goes awry when she is apprehended at the train, yet thanks to remarkable luck (or is it coordination?), Nelly Varga, then a frantic car ride with Perry who has appeared out of nowhere, and finally Godfrey, "the Master of Ceremonies" (323), on the other side of the Channel, Juliet escapes to the Continent where she lives for another thirty years and has a son. (None of Juliet's time outside of England is relevant to the novel and so sparsely sketched.)

Much of the narrative leaves unanswered questions that might arise about the events of 1940 and 1950, although brief summations of the war years conclude the earlier section: Giselle, Cyril, and Clarissa are all killed in the war at different points (reference is often made to a pearl necklace Juliet wears in the postwar years—we learn she removed it from Clarissa's body when Juliet was called to make the identification); Perry is transferred to the Ministry of Information and later works for the BBC on the "Children's Hour" program; Godfrey went to France to interrogate Nazi officers and then to Nuremberg before disappearing until his return in 1950, and then is rumored to be abroad again (322). A similar smattering of information updates characters in the 1950 section. Atkinson's concern, though, is how actions in the past reverberate in the greatly changed political circumstances of 1950. The rapid shift in alliances that occurred between 1945 and 1950 is bewildering and inspires many early Cold War espionage novels such as *The Looking-Glass War* and others by Le Carré. Allies such as the Soviet Union, who were once supported, are now enemies, and enemies such as (West) Germany and Berlin are now allies. For "idealists" such as Juliet, realpolitik has trumped all. It seems a universal trait among members of the service, regardless of their allegiance, to view humanity cynically: Godfrey (63), Perry (98), Alleyne (105), and Fisher (315) all take a dim view; "no one is entirely innocent," says Alleyne, so Fisher is perhaps right to be "suspicious of everyone" (315). What is clear, though, is that the separation of us versus them, Allies versus Axis, of democratic and capitalist West versus totalitarian and communist East, is the creation of macronarratives that simplify individuals and their relationships. As events in the Phoney War and the existence of the fifth columnists, the Right Club, and similar groups make clear, Britain was far from the united nation standing alone. Within government, there were those who argued for appeasement and a peace with Hitler; within the Conservative Party, there was debate about the leadership. Both these concerns find their expression in Atkinson's narrative of the 1940 surveillance and subtly allow readers to date the novel's action. The Cold War situation, then, when Soviet spies and moles are being exposed, offers a parallel situation with highly placed functionaries in government and individuals, such as Juliet, working against the state to assist a foreign power. The reasons may be quite different, but the Manichean notion of monolithic virtue in conflict with monolithic evil is surely undermined. Juliet's return to Britain is no longer relevant in the current political situation; rather, her appearance is necessary to tie up loose ends, to end a narrative if you will. Amusingly, Mr. Fisher declares in his final interview with Juliet, "Come now, quite enough of exposition and explanation. We're not approaching the end of a novel, Miss Armstrong" (315), but, of course, we are—a characteristic self-reflexive moment distances us from the narrative and the character. Curiously, we cannot be sure of Juliet's last words, although her pondering what they might be when she hears of a BBC colleague's death puts us in mind of the question (255): Does she say, "This England" (4, 327), recalling John of Gaunt in Shakespeare's *Richard II* but also an outing with Perry (67)? Or does she say, "It's all right," recalling words of Godfrey's reassurance (13 and elsewhere), which is the phrase paramedics believe they hear (327)? Both link thematically to the book's narrative, but neither is certain.

Obviously, to imagine that all that happens is "all right" is to take the long view of history, and there is a kind of resignation expressed in Juliet's death that may recall the sentiment of the last lines in *A God in Ruins* relating Teddy's death (374). Dying, she reflects on the political changes that rendered Russia and Germany enemies and allies, "It was all such a waste of breath. War and peace. Peace and war. It would go on forever without end" (4). In *A God in Ruins,* human failing lies at the root of human suffering; its cause is unknown though Hopkins's "Spring and Fall" may, most eloquently, offer a reason. *Transcription* arrives at a similar place. Indeed, "no one is innocent."

Conclusion

In the few years between first proposing this project on Kate Atkinson's fiction and the final submission of the completed manuscript to the University of South Carolina Press, Kate Atkinson released two novels and a small collection of short stories. In a few years time, there will be more stories and more books. Perhaps that future work will move in another direction apart from those that have been discussed here. Critics, however, are proficient at assimilating new material into an existing body, so I think it unlikely that Atkinson's future work will radically alter the understanding of her fiction that has been presented in these pages. For the writer, though, every new book is a new departure and something quite fresh, and for readers every book is something to look forward to.

Atkinson's fiction has moved from work heavily influenced by her reading of other literature toward an engagement with history. Nothing, though, is wholly left behind, and we find continuities in themes and narrative practices through all her books. Self-reflexive narrative, allusiveness, and wit are characteristic of all the work while multiple narrative strands are employed to suggest the richness of story and experience.

Atkinson once described herself as a "lapsed Quaker" (Bunce 2000), as someone who does not believe in an afterlife of consequence. For her, meaning is found in narrative and all her efforts are aimed at finding the meaning that lurks in history and in the life of individuals. Juliet Armstrong is another quester, like Ruby Lennox, Isobel Fairfax, Effie Stuart-Murray, Jackson Brodie, Ursula Todd, and the rest. All pursue the meaning of their lives, which Atkinson's readers are taught to well understand and for which attentive readers are grateful.

NOTES

ONE: Understanding Kate Atkinson

1. A Coover story is obliquely referred to near the end of "Pleasureland," the last story in *Not the End of the World,* and Barthelme's name comes up in *Emotionally Weird* (317), while the phrase "unspeakable practices and unnatural acts" appears there in description (75). In *A God in Ruins,* Viola's fledgling writing career is described as "an unspeakable practice" (132). *Unspeakable Practices, Unnatural Acts* is the title of Donald Barthelme's 1968 story collection.

2. Parker provides the list on page 26, and it is reprinted in the Readers' Group Guide for *Not the End of the World* (8–10).

3. Criticism employing the "middlebrow" term has proliferated; see, for example, Botshon and Goldsmith's *Middlebrow Moderns* (2013) and Alison Light's *Forever England* (1991).

4. Atkinson made a similar observation in 2004 to Helen Brown in the *Telegraph.* Her comments on the Booker have the shade of irony over them because Hilary Mantel has since won the Booker twice, while Pat Barker won in 1995. Barker similarly faced considerable criticism from reviewers after *The Ghost Road* was selected over Rushdie (Shaddock 2006, 657).

5. "If nothing else, *Life* was a gamble for Atkinson, who has built her readership mainly on the back of a classic tough-guy detective, Jackson Brodie, hero of four previous novels. But it has paid off, partly with the help of a major social-media campaign and has finally put Atkinson at the top of the U.S. bestseller lists" (Barber 2013). No mention here of her earlier successes or the possibility that *Life After Life* might not have needed a social media campaign (why mention that?).

TWO: A Postmodern Trilogy?

1. These are not printed as footnotes at the bottom of pages but rather as separate chapters.

2. Gillian is uncharacteristically generous toward Ruby when Ruby goes to stay with her Aunt Babs following Pearl's death—Ruby has Gillian's Ladybird book, *Puppies and Kittens,* with her (103). Ruby is surprised by Gillian's actions, but readers come to recognize they stem from guilt.

3. Lewis Carroll's Alice books, Grace Slick's "White Rabbit," the 1971 young adult novel published anonymously but written by Beatrice Sparks, and Alice, Ruby's

great-grandmother whose story is in the "Footnotes." Quattrocento, a Renaissance art movement, is notably referred to in Yeats' "Among School Children": "Did Quattrocento finger fashion it / Hollow of cheek as though it drank the wind" (lines 26–27).

4. Tracy Hargreaves (2009) is particularly good on the contrast between the royal family's public celebration of the coronation of Elizabeth II in 1953 and the Lennox's family gathering to watch the event on television. Sinead McDermott's essay "Kate Atkinson's Family Romance: Missing Mothers and Hidden Histories in *Behind the Scenes at the Museum*" (2006) extends the point about how domestic and national celebrations are contrasted with reference to the comic farce that is a family wedding reception that occurs during the 1966 World Cup final—the last time England won the World Cup.

5. This extreme act finally gets Ruby psychiatric attention. Similarly, in *Life After Life,* Ursula doesn't see a doctor until she pushes Bridget, the housemaid, down a flight of stairs.

6. Freud exemplified the experience of delayed trauma by describing the phenomenon in terms of a railway accident in *Moses and Monotheism* (84). Luckhurst summarizes the etiology of the railway accident in the nineteenth century (2008, 21–23).

7. For instance, "The television set is George's gift to Bunty, a consolation for having to bring up her family Above the Shop instead of a normal home" (71). Tellingly, Bunty sees little of the coronation because she is so busy attending to guests.

8. The scant details of Sophia's life here later give shape to Sylvie's background in *Life After Life;* even a family clock recurs there and in *God in Ruins.*

9. Further discussion of these interrelationships can be found in Julie Sanders's chapter, "Kate Atkinson in the House of Arden," in *Novel Shakespeares: Twentieth-Century Women Novelists and Appropriation* (2001, 66–83), and in Kevin Paul Smith's "Architextual/Chronotopic Intertextuality and Magic Realism in Kate Atkinson's *Human Croquet,*" in *The Postmodern Fairytale: Folkloric Intertexts in Contemporary Fiction* (2007, 57–86).

10. As is well known, Shakespeare willed his "second-best bed" to his wife, Anne Hathaway, and the forest of Arden is the setting of *As You Like It.*

11. "Intertextuality" has been well developed by theorists since the 1960s, but Mikhail Bakhtin did much of his most influential work between the wars in Soviet Russia, so it was largely unknown to English-speaking scholars until much later. His essay "Discourse in the Novel" is a good starting point for interested readers. Julia Kristeva's book *Desire in Language,* especially its essay "Word, Dialogue, and Novel," explores some of Bakhtin's thought. Roland Barthes's work frequently invokes the concept of intertextuality, but his essays "From Work to Text" and "The Death of the Author" offer clear discussions of often complex ideas.

12. Kevin Paul Smith discusses the relationships among the terms (2007, 83–86).

13. As Maria Tatar and others have observed, a less popular variant of the "Cinderella" story involves the father's incestuous desire for his daughter, whose escape is facilitated by a benevolent "fairy." His desire provides one motive for the stepmother's hostility toward the stepdaughter (1987, 149–51).

14. For readers, the experience is not déjà vu but *déjà lu,* as Barthes says.

15. In *Emotionally Weird,* Professor Cousins suggests "erythrophobia," fear of blushing, as an example in a word game (315). The catalog of fears speaks to Eunice's character as a kind of know-it-all but such fears are close to Atkinson's experience who suffered from a year of agoraphobia in the early 1990s that she overcame largely by reading (Teeman 2008; Clark 2001).

16. Any number of examples could be mentioned, but in Coover's story, "The Hat Act," from *Pricksongs and Descants* a magician can pull anything out of his hat. Coover, along with Barthelme, is one of those "writers who made me want to be a writer myself" (from the ten books *Guardian* list; rpt. in *Not the End of the World,* as part of the "Reading Group Guide" where the comment appears on page 9).

17. "'That's a great deal to make one word mean,' Alice said in a thoughtful tone. 'When I make a word do a lot of work like that,' said Humpty Dumpty, 'I always pay it extra.' 'Oh!' said Alice. She was much too puzzled to make any other remark. 'Ah, you should see 'em come round me of a Saturday night,' Humpty Dumpty went on, wagging his head gravely from side to side: 'for to get their wages, you know.'" (*Emotionally Weird,* xi).

THREE: Short Fiction

1. "Kate Atkinson's Top Ten Books," *Guardian* March 20, 2000, https://www.theguardian.com/books/2000/mar/20/bestbooks.fiction. The other books she identified are F. Scott Fitzgerald's *The Great Gatsby,* Kurt Vonnegut's *Slaughterhouse-Five,* Jane Austen's *Pride and Prejudice,* Richmal Crompton's *Just William,* Henry James's *What Maisie Knew,* Lewis Carroll's *Alice in Wonderland* and *Through the Looking-Glass,* Vladimir Nabokov's *Lolita,* George Eliot's *Middlemarch,* Mark Twain's *Huckleberry Finn,* and Ford Madox Ford's The Good Soldier is added. In total, her top-ten list actually includes more than thirteen titles (Crompton's *Just William* is a series of books).

2. Atkinson is constant in her praise of the Alice books and the role they played in her life and work. See, for example, E. Jane Dickson, "Sanity through the Looking Glass" (2001) and *Globe and Mail,* "Author Kate Atkinson: 'Alice in Wonderland' was my touchstone of all things wondrous" (2018).

3. The year here is often misreported, as it is in Parker's book, as 1988.

4. *Festive Spirits* contains "Small Mercies," but the book's copyright page notes that "St. Lucy's Day," another in the volume, appeared previously in *Good Housekeeping* and "Festive Spirits" in *The Independent.* "Small Mercies" is not credited to prior publication, but Parker cites it as previously appearing in *Good Housekeeping* in 2001. One can sometimes find issues that published some of Atkinson's stories available online for purchase. My one success in this regard was to find *You Magazine* (January 7, 1996) containing "This Dog's Life."

5. My intention is to tell of bodies changed / To different forms; the gods, who made the changes, / Will help me-or so I hope—with a poem / That runs from the world's beginning to our own days (trans. Rolfe Humphries).

6. Now I have done my work. It will endure, / I trust, beyond Jove's anger, fire, and sword, / Beyond Time's hunger. The day will come, I know, / So let it come, that day

which has no power / Save over my body, to end my span of life / Whatever it may be. Still, part of me, / The better part, immortal, will be borne / Above the stars; my name will be remembered" (trans. Rolfe Humphries). These are from the epilogue—nearly the last lines of the work.

7. http://www.barcelonareview.com/32/e_ka.htm.

FOUR: Detective Fiction

1. Todorov's *Poetics of Prose* contains his very influential "The Typology of Detective Fiction" (1977, 42–52).

2. *Trouble is My Business* is the title of one of Raymond Chandler's story collections.

3. Jackson's sister is killed in 1971; in *Case Histories* Jackson mentions in conversation with Kim Strachan, whom he's interviewing as part of an investigation, that it's "thirty-three years since [his] sister died" (250).

4. The television production of *Case Histories*—the general name for six episodes over two seasons in 2011 and 2013—includes two episodes after the fourth, which is *Started Early, Took My Dog.* These last two episodes, "Nobody's Darling" and "Jackson and the Women," were written for television by Emily Ballou and Debbie O'Malley, respectively. Kate Atkinson was a consultant for the series *Case Histories* but did not adapt or write for it.

5. The road rage scene might recall another accident early in Ian McEwan's *Saturday* (2005). Similarly, the final confrontation with Smith in *One Good Turn* echoes the final confrontation between Henry Perowne and Baxter in *Saturday,* which takes place in Perowne's living room before his family in a scene that reveals his daughter's pregnancy. In Atkinson's novel, though, the revelation of a pregnancy is deferred for a couple of chapters. Jackson's speculations about "lawyers, guns, and money" recall a song by Warren Zevon.

6. In *One Good Turn,* we are told that she went straight into the police after graduating, but in *When Will There Be Good News?* we find out "Louise had an MA in literature" (70). Presumably, Louise did some graduate courses between the two books, unless this is an oversight.

7. Gloria, like Isobel, also ponders clichéd expressions: "Dead as a doornail. Why a doornail? Why was a doornail deader than anything else? . . . did dead exist in the comparative? Could something be deader than something else? Dead, deader, deadest" (302). Ovid is also mentioned in *When Will There Be Good News?* (255).

8. The range of allusions in these quoted passages is quite wide: Edgar Allan Poe's "Fall of the House of Usher" and "The Masque of the Red Death"; M. Night Shyamalan's *The Sixth Sense;* J. B. Priestley's play *An Inspector Calls;* Agatha Christie's *The Murder of Roger Ackroyd;* and an echo of "Another Brick in the Wall" by Pink Floyd.

FIVE: War and Other Things

1. The Blitz refers to the sustained German bombing campaign against British cities from September 7, 1940, to May 10, 1941, which was considered preparatory to the

eventual invasion of Britain. Some sources, such as the Imperial War Museum (London) website (Amanda Mason, "The Blitz around Britain," IWM, January 8, 2018, https://www.iwm.org.uk/history/the-blitz-around-britain) but others as well, report that London endured fifty-seven consecutive nights of bombings from September 7 onward. This would mean that the Argyll Road bombing, which is recounted four times in the novel, occurs on the last night of this consecutive stretch. The end of the Blitz did not mean the end of aerial bombings against Britain, which continued with various levels of intensity throughout the war. About 43,000 civilians were killed and 139,000 injured during the Blitz (Adrian Gilbert, "The Blitz," *Encyclopaedia Brittanica*, https://www.britannica.com/event/the-Blitz).

2. Dr. Fellowes's misogyny is also apparent in his callous response to Sylvie's grief over Teddy's death from influenza: "Dear God, Dr Fellowes thought, the woman grieved like a savage" (102). He is equally hard-hearted in his consideration of traumatized veterans. Hearing of a man who in 1921 killed his wife and three children before shooting himself, Fellowes says, "Terrible mess. . . . These chaps should think about the people who have to clean up afterwards" (167–68).

3. Very early in the novel we learn that Hugh is absent when Ursula is born because he has gone to the Continent to fetch his sister who at sixteen had run off, pregnant, with a married man. For most of the book we understand that Hugh arranged for the child to be adopted in Germany (64, 384), but Izzie never mentions the baby and Ursula only learns of him when Izzie confides her distress that he may now be the "enemy" (384).

4. Ursula's experience recalls an episode, "Earshot," of *Buffy, the Vampire Slayer,* in which Buffy is overwhelmed by hearing multiple voices. The series is often mentioned as a favorite of Atkinson in profiles (see Cox 2002, for example) and noted occasionally in her fiction (for example, in "Transparent Fiction" and in "Temporal Anomaly" in *Not the End of the World,* 59 and 207, respectively).

5. Curiously, because there are no further references to the incident, in the narrative that involves Nancy's murder (August 1926), Ursula and Teddy find the body of another young girl a few years before (in December 1923). Sylvie is distressed because no one seemed to miss the child (174). In commenting on Nancy after the publication of *Life After Life,* Atkinson, who was already working on *A God in Ruins,* said suddenly to Sarah Lyall (2013), "I think Nancy's doomed."

6. Atkinson's "Note from the Author" explains that the Argyll Road bombing is invention and that she did get some details of the location wrong. On the other hand, the Aldwych rocket attack was a real event in June 1944.

7. It is curious to observe that while the Blitz, Dunkirk, and Bletchley Park are signature events in Britain's national tale, D-day is not: that moment, commanded by Eisenhower, has been absorbed into American myth.

8. Graham Greene mocks these hierarchies in *The End of the Affair* (1980b) where Bendrix considers how a small review will judge him: "Patronizingly in the end he would place me—probably a little above Maugham because Maugham is popular and I have not yet committed that crime—not yet" (148). Greene's 1951 novel makes the Blitz central to its plot. An earlier book, *The Ministry of Fear,* also dealt with the Blitz and included as a

crucial aspect of the protagonist's past the mercy killing of his wife. Atkinson is surely familiar with these texts. Late in *Life After Life,* Greene's *The Comedians* is Ursula's bedtime reading (427).

9. Stephanie Merritt's (2015) review of the novel noted Atkinson's joke as well. Perhaps another is found when we read about Viola starting out as a novelist: "Like all writing, it was a secretive act. And unspeakable practice" (132). *Unspeakable Practices, Unnatural Acts* is, again, the title of Donald Barthelme's 1968 story collection.

10. Perhaps it is the word "nightmares," but its occurrence and the situation echoes Isobel's and Charles's night in the woods and the discovery of their mother's body in *Human Croquet* (117).

11. "Time is a big part of much of my writing. I think an obsession with time is related to the fluidity and elasticity of fiction—fiction doesn't—or doesn't have to—obey the rules of physics and our 'real' lives" ("Baileys Women's Prize," n.d.).

12. These questions are central to several novels, but it is worth mentioning that one of them, *Slaughterhouse-Five,* is named by Atkinson as one of her top reads. The book is referred to by Viola in her accusations against her father (58).

13. The memorial at Runnymede, which Teddy visits, was dedicated in 1953 and commemorates the men and women from the Commonwealth nations who served in the RAF and other air forces in many roles.

14. Sturken, for instance, notes that items left at the Vietnam Memorial Wall are gathered and archived and that a network of veterans has worked to discover/uncover the meaning of cryptic messages and emblems that reflect on unknown aspects of that war's history (1997, 80–81).

15. In 1992 the Canadian Broadcasting Corporation (CBC) aired a three-part documentary, *The Valour and the Horror.* The second part was about Bomber Command and proved controversial. The Canadian Senate held hearings on the program in response to an outcry from veterans. And the Canadian war museum altered wording in its display devoted to the bombing campaign. When the show aired in Britain in the following year, similar protests from veterans' groups were heard, and the Queen Mother, patron of Bomber Command, sought unsuccessfully to prevent the show from airing. "Canadian War Museum Changes Controversial Wording on WWII Bombing," *CBC,* October 11, 2007, https://www.cbc.ca/news/entertainment/canadian-war-museum-changes-controversial-wording-on-wwii-bombing-1.635963. See also Bercuson and Wise (1994).

16. What might have motivated Teddy's action is not clear in *A God in Ruins,* although Whitman's "When Lilacs Last in the Dooryard Bloomed," one of the poet's elegies for Lincoln, may be in Atkinson's thoughts.

17. "Sowed the wind" reportedly originates with Arthur Harris, Head of Bomber Command, who said while watching a raid on the night of December 29, 1940, "They are sowing the wind" (Hansen 30).

18. The bombing of Hamburg in the last week of July 1943, called Operation Gomorrah (278), involved American and British raids for eight days and seven nights, with July 27 being the heaviest. About 42,000 people were killed—almost as many who died in the London Blitz.

19. In *Case Histories,* Caroline ponders the artifacts in a church, "but none of those

artifacts could express how you *felt*" (93)—hence the importance of literature to communicate meaning and feeling.

20. This frustrates Viola, who is insulted when Teddy returns a new oven from Siemens that she had purchased for him. Teddy, however, remembers that Siemens manufactured the crematoria used in the death camps (129; part of the "and so on" that justified the Nuremburg raid [also 340]).

21. This is a curious detail; interestingly, in Nancy Mitford's comic novel about espionage during the Phoney War, *Pigeon Pie* (1940), German spies in Britain kidnap Sophia Garfield's dog, Millie, to ensure Sophia's cooperation.

22. Juliet steals a Sevres teacup from Mrs. Scaife's, and the fact that it is Sevres is noted in several places. In "Charlene and Trudi Go Shopping" a Sevres bowl is stolen by Trudi. Elsewhere, Juliet imagines her seductive appeal in terms that recall Ruby Lennox's assertions of identity: "I am a gift. An apple waiting to be plucked. A rose. A pearl" (*Transcription*, 124, similarly 71 and 147), and when the agent Hartley and Juliet retrace their steps in search of a Czech scientist, they look over the less public parts of the hotel: "Juliet caught a brief glimpse of the world behind the scenes" (233); on the same page we find Juliet telling Hartley that she "used to work as a chambermaid in a hotel" and a reference to their "trail of breadcrumbs," both of which can be seen as alluding to Atkinson's earlier work.

23. "Certainly I was using straightforward allegorical ideas in parts of *Nights At the Circus*. Mignon, for example, is supposed to be Europe, the unfortunate, bedraggled orphan—Europe after the war—which is why she carries such a weight of literary and musical references on her frail shoulders" (qtd. in Haffenden 1985, 87).

24. "Hypocaust" is a term used in English (it refers to a system of heating beneath the floor of a room), but there's little doubt that the word unsaid guides readers toward "holocaust."

25. Similar constructions abound: "'I get hay fever.' She didn't (69)" or, "'Do you despair, Miss Armstrong?' Hardly ever. Occasionally. Quite often. 'No, not at all,' she said" (225), or, "'Is he expecting you?' 'Yes.' Of course, he wasn't" (241)—to give only three examples.

26. When Juliet enters the shop, she finds no one to greet her so she open and closes the door a second time so that its bell will ring. When this, too, fails to rouse a clerk, she calls, "Shop!" (238), which recalls the habits of the Lennox family in *Behind the Scenes at the Museum*, who call similarly when they enter the family pet shop.

27. As Graham Greene points out in "The Virtue of Disloyalty," every English schoolchild knows the lines (608).

28. In reflecting on Schools' programming, Juliet thinks, "Schools seemed to be fixated on an Old England of sea shanties and ballads and folk songs. And maidens, lots of maidens" (207). Given the period this is set, 1950 with the Festival of Britain to occur in the following year, a reconstructed image of England emphasizing historical continuity through the pastoral is very much part of the period's discourse.

29. As Atkinson notes, some of MI5's work in the novel has historical precedent. Vanderkamp, for instance, has a parallel in Tyler Kent who worked as cypher clerk at the American Embassy.

30. The funeral scene might recall Harry Lime's supposed internment near the opening of Graham Greene's *The Third Man.* Later, in an oblique reference to Greene's novella, we are told that immediately after the war, Hartley was stationed in Vienna: "It was a complete hell hole. Mind you, you could buy anything, there was nothing that didn't have a price. You couldn't *trust* anyone though" (201–2).

31. The urgency to choose sides was well felt in the 1930s and beyond. Juliet's debate with Mr. Fisher has a precursor in Greene's *The Confidential Agent* (1980a) where D. is challenged: "'Do you believe,' she said, 'that *your* leaders are any better than L.'s?' . . . 'No. Of course not. But I still prefer the people they lead—even if they lead them all wrong.' 'The poor right or wrong,' she scoffed. 'It's no worse—is it?—than my country, right or wrong. You choose your side once for all—of course, it may be the wrong side. Only history can tell that'" (60). At the end of this novel, D. is smuggled across the Channel out of England on a tramp steamer.

32. Published in early 1950, *The God That Failed* is a classic early Cold War text in which six prominent intellectuals describe their attraction to and then rejection of communism and the Communist Party. Edited by Richard Crossman, a prominent Labour Party member, the book became important in Cold War debate and remains in print. Nowhere is it suggested that Juliet was a party member, but her disavowal, "I no longer believe," clearly aligns her with the contributors to Crossman's book.

33. Hartley had been stationed in Vienna, and it is worth noting that Kim Philby was stationed there from 1933 to 1934, when, he writes, he became devoted to the Soviet cause (Knightley 2002, xxx–xxxi; Philby 2002, 203–4).

34. Greene's address on being awarded the "Shakespeare Prize" at the University of Hamburg argues writers must stand in opposition to power and align themselves with the victims in society, hence the "disloyalty" of writers.

35. Atkinson finds Dee's review puzzling (Brown 2018).

BIBLIOGRAPHY

Works by Kate Atkinson

Abandonment (2000). London: Nick Hern Books, 2011.

"Affairs of the Heart" (2008). In *Crimespotting: An Edinburgh Crime Collection,* ed. Irvine Welsh, 13–34. Edinburgh: Polygon, 2009.

Behind the Scenes at the Museum. 1995; repr., New York: Picador, 1996.

Big Sky. New York: Doubleday Canada, 2019.

Case Histories. 2004; repr., London: Back Bay, 2005.

Emotionally Weird: A Comic Novel. 2000; repr., London: Black Swan, 2001.

A God in Ruins. New York: Doubleday Canada, 2015.

Human Croquet. London: Doubleday, 1997.

"Inner Balance." *Barcelona Review,* no. 32, September–October 2002. http://www.barcelonareview.com/32/e_ka.htm.

Introduction to *Pricksongs and Descants* by Robert Coover. London: Penguin Classics, 2011.

"Karmic Mothers-Fact or Fiction?" *Snapshots: Winning Stories from the First 10 Years of the Ian St James Awards,* 156–163. Tunbridge Wells, Kent: Angela Royal, 1999.

Life After Life. Toronto: Anchor Canada, 2013.

"Lucky We Live Now." *Scotsman.* July 2, 2009. https://www.scotsman.com/arts-and-culture/books/exclusive-short-story-lucky-we-live-now-kate-atkinson-2461425.

"Night in the Museum: Kate Atkinson on the Origins of *Behind the Scenes at the Museum.*" *Guardian,* November 1, 2008. https://www.theguardian.com/books/2008/nov/01/atkinson.

Not the End of the World. 2002. "Reading Group Guide," appended. New York: Back Bay, 2004.

One Good Turn: A Jolly Murder Mystery. 2006; repr., Toronto: Anchor Canada, 2007.

"*Pricksongs & Descants,* Robert Coover." In *The Book That Changed My Life: 71 Remarkable Writers Celebrate the Books That Matter Most to Them,* ed. Roxanne J. Coady and Joy Hohannessen, 4–6. New York Gotham, 2006.

"Putting the Fun Back into Fiction: Short Stories Were a Breath of Fresh Air for Kate Atkinson." *Guardian,* June 21, 2003. https://www.theguardian.com/books/2003/jun/21/featuresreviews.guardianreview27.

Started Early, Took My Dog. New York: Doubleday Canada, 2010.

"To Die For." *Guardian,* March 28, 2009. https://www.theguardian.com/books/2009/mar/28/die-for-kate-atkinson-story.

Transcription. Toronto: Bond Street, 2018.

"The War on Women." In *Freedom: A Collection of Short Fiction Celebrating the Universal Declaration of Human Rights*, 216–33. London: Amnesty International; Toronto: Key Porter.

When Will There Be Good News? Toronto: Anchor Canada, 2009.

Interviews, Reviews, and Other References

Aitkenhead, Decca. 1996. "A New Chapter Begins in the Maid's Story." *Independent* (UK), January 28. https://www.independent.co.uk/news/uk/home-news/a-new-chapter-begins-in-the-maids-story-1326185.html.

Andermahr, Sonya. 2013. "'Compulsively Readable and Deeply Moving': Women's Middlebrow Trauma Fiction." In *Trauma Narratives and Herstory*, edited by Sonya Andermahr and Silvia Pellicer-Ortin, 13–29. Basingstoke, UK: Palgrave Macmillan.

Arias, Rosario. 2015. "Telling Otherwise: Collective and Personal Remembering and Forgetting in Kate Atkinson's *Life After Life*." *Prospero: Rivista di letterature e culture straniere*, December 21. https://dx.doi.org/10.13137/2283-6438/11872.

Atkinson, Kate. 2019. *Festive Spirit: Three Short Stories*. London: Doubleday.

———. "To Die For." In *Midsummer Nights*, edited by Jeanette Winterson, 43–65. Repr., London: Quercus, 2009.

Baileys Women's Prize for Fiction. N.d. "A Q&A with Kate Atkinson." https://www.womensprizeforfiction.co.uk/reading-room/blog-old/interviews-old/a-qa-with-kate-atkinson. Accessed February 8, 2019.

Bal, Mieke. 1999. Introduction to *Acts of Memory: Cultural Recall in the Present*. Ed. Mieke Bal, Jonathan Crewe, and Leo Spitzer, vii–xvii. Hanover, N.H.: University Press of New England.

Barber, John. 2013. "Kate Atkinson Leaves Her Detective Tales Behind—and the Gamble Pays Off." *Globe and Mail*. April 23. https://www.theglobeandmail.com/arts/books-and-media/kate-atkinson-leaves-her-detective-tales-behind-and-the-gamble-pays-off/article11501317/.

Barthes, Roland. 1974. *S/Z: An Essay*. 1970. Trans. Richard Howard. New York: Hill and Wang.

———. 1994. *Camera Lucida: Reflections on Photography* (1980). Trans. Richard Howard. 1981; repr., New York: Hill and Wang.

Bercuson, David J., and S. F. Wise, eds. 1994. *Valour and the Horror Revisited*. Montreal: McGill-Queen's University Press.

Blunt, Jax. 2015. "An Interview with Kate Atkinson, and Some Thoughts on *A God in Ruins*." *Making It Up as We Go Along* (blog), May 13. https://liveotherwise.co.uk/makingitup/2015/05/13/an-interview-with-kate-atkinson-and-some-thoughts-on-a-god-in-ruins/.

Botshon, Lisa, and Meredith Goldsmith, eds. 2013. *Middlebrow Moderns: Popular Women Writers of the 1920s*. Boston: Northeastern University Press.

British Council. N.d. "Kate Atkinson." https://literature.britishcouncil.org/writer/kate-atkinson. Accessed February 8, 2019.

Brooks, Peter. 1984. *Reading for the Plot: Design and Intention in Narrative.* New York: Vintage.

Brown, Helen. 2004. "A Writer's Life: Kate Atkinson." *Telegraph,* August 29. https://www.telegraph.co.uk/culture/books/3622950/A-writers-life-Kate-Atkinson.html.

Brown, Mark. 2018. "Kate Atkinson Calls Authors Reviewing Their Peers a Callous Art." *Guardian,* October 7. https://www.theguardian.com/books/2018/oct/07/kate-atkinson-calls-authors-reviewing-their-peers-a-callous-art-transcription.

Bunce, Kim. 2000. "Emotionally Weird? Moi?: Kim Bunce Interviews Whitbread-Winning Author Kate Atkinson about God, Motherhood and the Uncontrolled Imagination." *Guardian,* March 12. https://www.theguardian.com/books/2000/mar/12/fiction.features.

Butki, Scott. 2011. "An Interview with Kate Atkinson, Author of *Started Early, Took My Dog.*" *Seattle PI,* May 16. https://www.seattlepi.com/lifestyle/blogcritics/article/An-Interview-With-Kate-Atkinson-Author-of-1381960.php.

By the Book. 2018. "Kate Atkinson: By the Book." *New York Times,* September 6. https://www.nytimes.com/2018/09/06/books/review/kate-atkinson-by-the-book.html.

Carter, Angela. 1994. *Nights at the Circus.* 1984; repr., London: Vintage.

Caruth, Cathy. 1996. *Unclaimed Experience: Trauma, Narrative, and History.* Baltimore: Johns Hopkins University Press.

Clark, Alex. 2001. "The Fragility of Goodness: Kate Atkinson Tells Alex Clark How She Overcame Her Nerves." *Guardian,* March 10. https://www.theguardian.com/books/2001/mar/10/fiction.alexclark.

Cox, Tom. 2002. "Like Buffy but More Huffy." *Times,* November 2. https://www.thetimes.co.uk/article/like-buffy-but-more-huffy-npz5v8cdw6m.

Craig, Amanda. 2006. "*One Good Turn* by Kate Atkinson." *Independent.* August 18. https://www.independent.co.uk/arts-entertainment/books/reviews/one-good-turn-by-kate-atkinson-412292.html.

Dee, Jonathan. 2018. "Kate Atkinson's Spy Novel Makes the Genre New." *New Yorker,* September 24. https://www.newyorker.com/magazine/2018/09/24/kate-atkinsons-spy-novel-makes-the-genre-new.

Dickson, E. Jane. 2001. "Sanity through the Looking Glass: In a World of Inexplicable Adults, Kate Atkinson Looked to *Alice in Wonderland* for an Explanation . . ." *Times,* February 24. http://www.geocities.ws/kateatkinson14/alice.htm.

Doyle, Arthur Conan. 1930. *The Complete Sherlock Holmes.* 2 vols. Garden City, N.Y.: Doubleday.

Fox, Genevieve. 2011. "Kate Atkinson: Week One Interview." *Telegraph,* June 30. https://www.telegraph.co.uk/culture/books/bookreviews/8608641/Kate-Atkinson-Week-One-Interview.html.

Freud, Sigmund. *Moses and Monotheism.* Trans. Katherine Jones. 1939. New York: Vintage, 1958.

Globe and Mail. 2018. "Author Kate Atkinson: *Alice in Wonderland* Was My Touchstone of All Things Wondrous." May 11, 2015. Updated May 18, 2018. https://www.theglobeandmail.com/arts/books-and-media/author-kate-atkinson-alice-in-wonderland-was-my-touchstone-of-all-things-wondrous/article24366223/.

Goodreads. 2018. "Interview with Kate Atkinson." September 6. https://www.goodreads.com/interviews/show/1389.Kate_Atkinson.

Greene, Graham. 1973. "The Virtue of Disloyalty." In *The Portable Graham Greene*, edited by Philip Stratford, 606–60. New York: Viking.

———. 1980a. *The Confidential Agent*. 1939; repr., Harmondworth, England: Penguin.

———. 1980b. *The End of the Affair*. 1951; repr., Harmondsworth, England: Penguin.

Haffenden, John. 1985. *Novelists in Interview*. London: Methuen.

Hansen, Randall. *Fire and Fury: The Allied Bombing of Germany 1942–45*. Np: Doubleday, 2008.

Hargreaves, Tracy. 2009. "Redressing the Queen's Two Bodies in Kate Atkinson's *Behind the Scenes at the Museum*." *Literature and History*, November 1. https://doi.org/10.7227%2FLH.18.2.4.

Hartman, Geoffrey. 1997. *The Fateful Question of Culture*. New York: Columbia University Press.

Hawkes, John, and John J. Enck. 1965. "John Hawkes: An Interview." *Wisconsin Studies in Contemporary Literature* 6, no. 2: 141–55. www.jstor.org/stable/1207254.

Hooker, Ginny. 2006. "Take a Leaf out of Their Books. [. . .] Writers and Critics Make Their Picks of 2006." *Guardian*, November 25. https://www.theguardian.com/books/2006/nov/25/bestbooksoftheyear.bestbooks.

Hühn, Peter. 1987. "The Detective as Reader: Narrativity and Reading Concepts in Detective Fiction." *Modern Fiction Studies* 33, no. 3 (Autumn): 451–66. https://www.jstor.org/stable/26282385.

Humble, Nicola. 2001. *The Feminine Middlebrow Novel, 1920s to 1950s: Class, Domesticity, and Bohemianism*. Oxford, England: Oxford University Press.

Jackson, Nicole. 2009. "The Book That Changed My Life: *Lolita*, the Bible, or *Dr No*? We Asked Writers to Reveal Their Literary Inspirations." Interviews by Nicole Jackson. *Guardian*, May 26. https://www.theguardian.com/books/2009/may/26/hay-festival-book-changed-life.

Jewell, Stephen. 2008. "Liberated by Her Own Inventions." *Weekend Australian*. August 23. https://www.theaustralian.com.au/arts/books/liberated-by-her-own-inventions/news-story/0c9449cfe3540f7d1b6d1fabd366348d.

NPR. 2015. "Kate Atkinson Tells Book Club How She Crafts Characters at All Life Stages." *Morning Edition Reads* book club. Transcript. June 16. https://www.npr.org/2015/06/16/414669606/kate-atkinson-tells-book-club-how-she-crafts-characters-at-all-life-stages.

Kauffman, Jeffrey. 2002. Introduction to *Loss of the Assumptive World: A Theory of Traumatic Loss*, 1–9. New York and London: Brunner-Routledge.

Knightley, Phillip. 2002. Introduction to *My Silent War: The Autobiography of a Spy* by Kim Philby, vii–xv. 1968; repr., New York: Modern Library.

Kristeva, Julia. 1982. *The Powers of Horror: An Essay on Abjection*. Trans. Leon S. Roudiez. 1980; repr., New York: Columbia University Press.

———. 1986. "Revolution in Poetic Language" (1974). Trans. Margaret Waller. *The Kristeva Reader*. Ed. Toril Moi, 90–136. Oxford, England: Basil Blackwell.

Lacan, Jacques. 1977. "The Mirror Stage as Formative of the Function of the I" (1949). In Écrits: *A Selection.* Trans, Alan Sheridan, 1–7. New York: Norton.

Laws, Alex. 2013a. "Q&A, Part 1: Kate Atkinson, Author of *Life After Life.*" *Chatelaine,* April 20. https://www.chatelaine.com/living/books/qa-part-1-kate-atkinson-author-of-life-after-life/.

———. 2013b. "What Every Wannabe Writer Needs to Know: Kate Atkinson, Author of *Life After Life,* on What It Takes to Be a Writer—and How Not Everyone Can Do It." *Chatelaine,* November 15. https://www.chatelaine.com/living/books/author-kate-atkinson-fiction-writing-tips-what-every-wannabe-writer-needs-to-know/.

———. 2013c. "Why Our Book Club Author Thinks Happiness Is Boring." *Chatelaine,* April 27. https://www.chatelaine.com/living/books/qa-part-2-kate-atkinson-author-of-life-after-life/.

Light, Alison. 1991. *Forever England: Femininity, Literature, and Conservativism between the Wars.* New York: Routledge.

Luckhurst, Roger. 2008. *The Trauma Question.* London: Routledge.

Lyall, Sarah. 2013. "Kate Atkinson's 'Groundhog Day' Fiction." *New York Times Magazine.* March 22. https://www.nytimes.com/2013/03/24/magazine/kate-atkinsons-groundhog-day-fiction.html.

Magwood, Michele. 2018. "In an Exclusive Interview, Kate Atkinson Talks to Michele Magwood about Spying, Brexit, and World War II." *Sunday Times,* September 17. http://bookslive.co.za/blog/2018/09/17/in-an-exclusive-interview-kate-atkinson-talks-to-michele-magwood-about-spying-brexit-and-world-war-ii/.

Mantel, Hilary. 1996. "Shop!" *London Review of Books,* April 4, pp. 23–24. https://www.lrb.co.uk.v18/n07/hilary-mantel/shop.

Maslin, Janet. 2015. "Review: Kate Atkinson's *A God in Ruins* Offers Lives Skipping among Eras." *New York Time,* April 30. https://www.nytimes.com/2015/05/01/books/review-kate-atkinsons-a-god-in-ruins-offers-lives-skipping-among-eras.html.

———. 2018. "In *Transcription,* Kate Atkinson Delivers a Story of Wartime Espionage." *New York Times,* September 16. https://www.nytimes.com/2018/09/16/books/review-transcription-kate-atkinson.html.

McDermott, Sinead. 2006. "Kate Atkinson's Family Romance: Missing Mothers and Hidden Histories in *Behind the Scenes at the Museum.*" *Critical Survey* 18, no. 2: 67–78.

Merritt, Stephanie. 2015. "*A God in Ruins* by Kate Atkinson Review—Her Finest Work." *Guardian,* May 10. https://www.theguardian.com/books/2015/may/10/a-god-in-ruins-kate-atkinson-observer-review.

Meyer, Sandra. 2010. "The Quest for Identity and Its Literary Representation through Metanarrative and Metafictional Elements in Kate Atkinson's *Emotionally Weird* and *Human Croquet.*" *English Studies* 91, no. 4 (June): 4430–56. https://dx.doi.org/10.1080/00138381003647624.

Micir, Melanie. 2017. "The Impossible Miss Woolf: Kate Atkinson and the Feminist Modernist Historical Novel." *Modern Language Quarterly* 78, no. 4 (December): 517–38. https://dx.doi.org/10.1215/00267929-4198253.

Morris, Linda. 2013. "The Interview: Kate Atkinson." *Sydney Morning Herald,* March 16. https://www.smh.com.au/entertainment/books/the-interview-kate-atkinson-20130313-2g0oz.html.

Mundler, Helen E. 2009. "Apoclypse and the Resurgence of the Creative Imagination in *Not the End of the World* by Kate Atkinson." *Journal of the Short Story in English* 52 (Spring). http://jsse.revues.org/975.

Ovid. 1972. *Metamorphoses.* Trans. Rolfe Humphries. 1952; repr., Bloomington: Indiana University Press.

Parker, Emma. 2002. *Kate Atkinson's "Behind the Scenes at the Museum."* London: Continuum Contemporaries.

Philby, Kim. 2002. *My Silent War: The Autobiography of a Spy.* 1968; repr., New York: Modern Library.

Prose, Francine. 2013. "Subject to Revision: *Life After Life,* by Kate Atkinson." *New York Times,* April 26. https://www.nytimes.com/2013/04/28/books/review/life-after-life-by-kate-atkinson.html.

Rankin, Ian. 2015. *Even Dogs in the Wild.* London: Orion.

Sanders, Julie. 2001. *Novel Shakespeares: Twentieth-Century Women Novelists and Appropriation.* Manchester, England: Manchester University Press.

———. 2010. *Adaptation and Appropriation.* 2006; repr., New York: Routledge.

Schudsun, Michael. 1993. *Watergate in American Memory: How We Remember, Forget, and Reconstruct the Past.* 1992; repr., New York: Basic.

Scribner, Amy. 2006. "Kate Atkinson: Scandal in Scotland." *BookPage* interview, October. https://bookpage.com/interviews/8372-kate-atkinson#.YYi_h-mQyUk.

Shaddock, Judith. 2006. "Dreams of Melanesia: Masculinity and the Exorcism of War in Pat Barker's *The Ghost Road.*" *Modern Fiction Studies* 52, no. 3 (Fall): 656–74. https://doi.org/10.1353/mfs.2006.0074.

Simon, Scott. 2013. "Author Interviews: *Life After Life,* The Many Deaths and Do-Overs of Ursula Todd." NPR, *Weekend Edition Saturday.* Transcript, March 28, 2013. https://www.npr.org/2013/03/30/175605206/life-after-life-the-many-deaths-and-do-overs-of-ursula-todd.

Smith, Kevin Paul. 2007. *The Postmodern Fairytale: Folkloric Intertexts in Contemporary Fiction.* New York: Palgrave Macmillan.

Stanton, Sally. 2004. "A Good Man Is Hard to Find: PW Talks to Kate Atkinson." *Publishers Weekly,* October 25. https://www.publishersweekly.com/pw/by-topic/authors/interviews/article/21587-a-good-man-is-hard-to-find.html Rpt. in *Case Histories,* 2005, "Reading Group Guide: Case Histories."

Stewart, Victoria. 2015. "The Second World War in Contemporary Women's Fiction: Revisiting the Home Front." *Contemporary Women's Writing* 9, no. 3 (November): 416–32. https://doi.org/10.1093/cww/vpv025.

Sturken, Marita. 1997. *Tangled Memories: The Vietnam War, The Aids Epidemic, and the Politics of Remembering.* Berkeley: University of California Press.

Swift, Graham. 1984. *Waterland.* 1983; repr., London: Picador.

Tatar, Maria. 1987. *The Hard Facts of the Grimm's Fairy Tales.* Princeton, N.J.: Princeton University Press.

Teeman, Tim. 2008. "Interview: Kate Atkinson: Behind the Scenes." *Times,* August 9. http://www.timteeman.com/2008/08/09/kate-atkinson-behind-the-scenes/.

Todorov, Tzvetan. 1977. *The Poetics of Prose.* Trans. Richard Howard. 1971; repr., Ithaca, N.Y.: Cornell University Press.

———. 1980. *The Fantastic: A Structural Approach to a Literary Genre.* Trans. Richard Howard. 1970; repr., Ithaca, N.Y.: Cornell University Press.

Tolan, Fiona. 2008. "Kate Atkinson" (Interview conducted July 11, 2006). In *Writers Talk: Conversations with Contemporary British Novelists.* Ed. Philip Tew, Fiona Tolan, and Leigh Wilson, 1–17. New York: Continuum.

———. 2009. "'Everyone has left something here': The Storyteller-Historian in Kate Atkinson's *Behind the Scenes at the Museum,*" *Critique: Studies in Contemporary Fiction* 50, no. 3: 275–92. https://dx.doi.org/10.3200/CRIT.50.3.275-292.

Toronto appearance. 2018. "Kate Atkinson in Conversation with Rachel Giese." Church of the Holy Trinity, Toronto. September 27.

van Alphen, Ernst. 1999. "Symptoms of Discursivity: Experience, Memory, and Trauma." In *Acts of Memory: Cultural Recall in the Present.* Ed. Mieke Bal, Jonathan Crewe, and Leo Spitzer, 24–38. Hanover, N.H.: University Press of New England.

Weber, Katharine. 1997. "The Best of All Parallel Worlds?" Review of *Human Croquet. New York Times,* July 6. http://movies2.nytimes.com/books/97/07/06/reviews/970706.06webbert.html.

White, Hayden. 1985. "The Fictions of Factual Representation." *Tropics of Discourse: Essays in Cultural Criticism,* 121–34. 1978; repr., Baltimore: Johns Hopkins University Press.

Whitehead, Anne. 2004. *Trauma Fiction.* Edinburgh: Edinburgh University Press.

Woolf, Virginia. 1961. "Middlebrow." In *"The Death of the Moth" and Other Essays,* 152–60. 1942; repr., Harmondsworth, England: Penguin.

———. 1984. "Modern Fiction" (1919). In *The Common Reader, First Series.* Ed. Andrew McNeillie, 146–54. 1925; repr., New York: Harcourt, Brace, Jovanovich.

INDEX